Seven Days Sober

A Guide to Discovering
What You Really Think About Your Drinking

by Meredith Bell

Green Rabbit Media
GreenRabbitMedia.com
info@greenrabbitmedia.com

This book is not intended as a substitute for the medical advice of physicians. The reader should regularly consult a physician in matters relating to his/her health and particularly with respect to any symptoms that may require diagnosis or medical attention.

Notes on the Expanded 2020 Edition

Our world has changed dramatically since I first published Seven Days Sober several years ago. As I write this, I am in quarantine in Sonoma County due to COVID-19, locked down in the same home I was forced to evacuate due to wildfires last fall. As of today, I still have my full-time job, but keeping it is looking less and less likely as the days go by and this shutdown takes its toll on our economy.

Two weeks ago, my brother died of a drug overdose. We started out the same way: teenage social boozers and partiers who turned into adult heavy drinkers. But while I fought to gain sobriety, his addiction to alcohol turned into a reliance on prescription pills, then street drugs and finally canned computer duster, which was the only high he could still afford. He left behind two kids and a wake of confusion and sadness.

I am acutely aware of how times of great stress can make us look at the world differently. As far as facing sobriety during times of crisis goes, there are basically two types of people: those who give up, grab their fuck-it bucket and head into alcohol-induced oblivion, and those who answer the wake-up call that leads to a better life. Which are you?

It's possible that you are profoundly disturbed by the chaos of our current situation and are feeling compelled to make a change that you *can* control. Sobriety could be that change.

You might be seeing the overwhelming emphasis in our media on using alcohol to cope—and you're thinking that maybe this is not the answer for you. Despite the fact that the WHO specifically released a statement making it clear that alcohol is not an acceptable coping strategy, talk of drinking is everywhere. Not only have liquor stores, wineries and breweries been designated "essential businesses," but your social media feeds are probably filled with jokes about cocktails and wine and beer being what we all need to get through this. If I see another mention of a "quarantini" I am personally going to lose it.

If you have relied on alcohol to handle your stress, you might have discovered that it's not really fixing anything. In fact, you've probably found that it's making everything worse.

If you're anxious, alcohol will make you more anxious. If you're depressed about a job loss or a sick relative, or worried about getting sick yourself, alcohol will make you more depressed. If you're feeling unhealthy, it's because drinking makes you unhealthy. If you're angry, alcohol has the potential to make you violent. If you're lonely, adding alcohol to the mix can lead to destructive decisions.

This book is not a magic cure-all for everything you are facing. But it does offer an achievable program to help you decide what role you want drinking to play in your life moving forward. The world is a scary place, and changing your relationship to alcohol is a deep, difficult process. But seven days is a small start that can lead to enormous shifts in your perspective.

Learning anything new is hard and takes a long time. But here's the thing. The time is going to pass whether or not you put the effort in to improve your life. Seven days will go by no matter what. How do you choose to spend those days? Drinking more and wondering why you can't stop? Or taking a pause to see what's behind your choices?

I invite you to at least consider, during this unique confluence of world events, that you are perfectly situated to change your life dramatically for the better. So many events and possibilities are outside of your direct control. But not this. The decision to get sober is up to you and you alone. I'm excited that you've picked up this book, and I know that if you take this well-deserved break from drinking, you will look back on this time as the beginning of an unimaginable journey.

Take care,

Meredith

Introduction

The first drink I ever had was a glass of white zinfandel my aunt poured for me when I was 14 years-old. My family had survived a harrowing whitewater adventure where our raft had flipped over and dumped us into a river swollen from four days of hurricane-level rains. My parents, my aunt and I had all nearly drowned. We became trapped by the raging river and were forced to hike several miles through the wilderness back to civilization.

The anxiety caused by the day's events made it difficult for me to fall asleep. But after I slugged back that glass of pink wine I had almost no trouble tripping off into dreamland. *Bliss*. My first experience with alcohol cemented in my mind that there was no quicker or better way for me to calm my nerves.

I continued to seek out opportunities to drink throughout my teens. My parents never kept any alcohol in the house, so I attached myself to friends who were able to procure alcohol for me, and I kept them close at hand. My drinking buddies weren't usually my best friends, but I sought them out and used them for their ability to get the alcohol I craved. I was far too chicken to get it myself.

I loved everything about drinking—the thrill of breaking the rules, the loopy conversations and tricking everyone's parents. I can honestly say I even enjoyed the taste of the cheap Milwaukee's Best beer (the Beast!) we passed around the campfire after football games on Friday nights. And I loved the way drinking made me feel. I was an overanxious overachiever (still am), and I suffered from a low-grade depression that ran in my family (still do). The numbing buzz I discovered while drinking was a shortcut to an instant relaxation that I simply couldn't find anywhere else.

Until I was in my mid-twenties I drank whenever I could, but my drinking stopped short of all-out destructive behavior. I considered myself a social drinker, and most of the people I drank with would have thought the same about me.

As fate would have it, I fell in love with and got married to a man who grew up in the Napa Valley wine industry, and we made our living making and marketing wine.

Drinking became a part of every aspect of my life. My work revolved around promoting wine, my nights and weekends were spent drinking it and every other activity in which I participated involved discovering, tasting, buying, storing, writing about and thinking about wine. It got to the point where I wouldn't consider doing anything unless wine was involved.

Going for a walk on the beach was tolerable only because there was a restaurant that poured one of my favorite chardonnays nearby. Working in my garden was an opportunity to sip in the sunshine while digging in the dirt. Shopping outings were punctuated by a stop at the wine bar. Meeting a friend for lunch turned into drinking until ten o'clock at night. I threw wild parties—the cops came to my house for noise complaints nine times over a period of two years.

My drinking escalated as my marriage fell apart. I don't think it takes an addiction expert to point out stress can escalate escapist behaviors. But I suffered from night sweats if I didn't have several drinks before bed. I shook in the morning because of the severity of my hangovers. I threw up any time I drank red wine after white (and then went right back to drinking). That's when I got real honest with myself that—even though I made no effort whatsoever to quit—my relationship with alcohol was officially destructive.

My first attempts to control my drinking included drinking water at parties until 9 p.m. in the hopes that I wouldn't get completely hammered. The result of that was, when 9 p.m. hit, I did all I could to catch up, and then drank until 2 a.m. *Fail.*

Then I cut out all hard alcohol. Then I only drank Thursdays through Saturdays. Then I tried the one glass of wine, one glass of water method. Then I gave up and drank what I wanted whenever I wanted, thinking I was a lost cause. On nights that I wasn't able to drink for one reason or the other I suffered sleeping difficulties, night sweats, panics and suicidal thoughts.

I knew I was a problem drinker long before I was able to tell anyone. And I knew it, really *knew* it, many years before I took *any real action* to quit.

Part of my problem with alcohol was that, since I made my living in wine for so long, my suggestion that I might need to cut back on my drinking was met with resistance. No one would accept that I had a problem because this level of drinking was normal in our circle. I begged my husband to pay for rehab, but he refused. Drinking was part of our lifestyle, he said, and I just needed to learn to control myself.

I tried to control myself, but the fact was that I was addicted to alcohol and I needed more than willpower to pull myself together.

You may not work in the wine and spirits industry, but since you picked up this book, I'm guessing that drinking is "part of your lifestyle," too. You might be questioning how much alcohol is affecting your work, relationships, energy level and wallet. You might wonder what your life would look like if you quit drinking for a while.

I've worked one-on-one with a therapist, I've gone to Alcoholics Anonymous meetings and read every book that had anything to do with drinking. I've participated in hypnotherapy to learn how to relax without chemicals. I've exercised. I've meditated. It's been a long, lonely process to get to the point where I it is actually my choice to drink or not. Because even though I was successful, well-liked, DUI-free and a happy-seeming drunk, the undeniable truth is that, for over a decade, I drank because I *had to*.

What I've realized from this thorough study is that one of my barriers for quitting drinking is the prevailing wisdom (and good advice in most cases) that in order for me to control my drinking I must never, ever drink again.

I'm a disciplined person, and I rarely shy away from a challenge. But I've found that this "never" thinking actually kept me from quitting. Looking out at the rest of my life without a drink was too daunting—at the beginning. The AA folks wisely take things "one day at a time" for this very reason. But I had projected that "one day at a time" to be a soul-crushing, endless march of joyless days. And the fact that I kept drinking while pondering this made me even less likely to make a change. **Daily drinking in any amount affects your ability to think and reason.**

That's why I wrote *Seven Days Sober*. If you're a daily drinker who is concerned about how drinking is affecting your life, I propose that you take a weeklong break from drinking to determine your next steps. Seven days is a manageable amount of time that will allow you to take a breather from drinking in order to give yourself an opportunity to evaluate your drinking with a clear head.

This book is not about encouraging everyone in the world to quit drinking. It's not even about encouraging *you* to quit drinking. What this guide will do is allow you a thoughtful time out in order to help you arrive at a complete understanding of your relationship with alcohol. Or, more simply, you'll have some time—just for you—to dip a toe into an alcohol-free pool to see if it suits you.

This book is not designed to be a substitute for a legitimate alcohol rehabilitation program. *Seven Days Sober* is a brief guide to taking a break from drinking so you can evaluate whether or not your current level of drinking works in your life. **If you are experiencing painful withdrawals, vomiting, sweats, dehydration, dark thoughts, hallucinations or any other physical or mental issues as a result of stopping drinking, seek medical help immediately.**

This is not something to be taken lightly—people die from alcohol withdrawal.

If you have a drinking habit that is overshadowing your life, if you have had recurring legal troubles as a result of your drinking, if you are isolated and alone, *Seven Days Sober* may not be the plan for you. I encourage anyone to seek professional help at any time during the course of the book, be it right now or when the *Seven Days Sober* journey is complete.

If you're a social drinker, a binge drinker or someone who is curious what life might be like without your nightly vodka tonic, give *Seven Days Sober* a try. What you decide to do about your drinking at the end of the week is up to you. You may discover that the amount you drink is perfectly fine for your goals and your lifestyle. You may learn that you have a more serious problem that requires treatment. Or you may find that living alcohol-free is an effortless choice and decide to never uncork a bottle again. The point is that it's your decision.

Like anything that we're motivated to do, the enthusiasm out of the gate makes the early days a snap. The first few days may be a breeze for you, and that's great! But you could start to hit some emotional walls. You might feel that, since you've had success instantly, you can "reward" yourself with a drink because you've been so disciplined.

I encourage you to stick with sobriety for seven days. You can read the entire book at once, or you can take it day by day. Be sure to check out the Special Section at the end that includes Sixty Things to Do While You're Not Drinking. There are several great suggestions in there for how to fill the time that's been left empty now that you're not drinking.

Read all the pages. Answer all the questions. Take the advice. Use the Special Section. When you've reached your eighth day, you may decide to reach for a drink—or you may walk away from alcohol for good. But I promise you that your perspective on drinking, and the role that drinking plays in your life, will be dramatically different no matter what your decision.

In Sobriety,

Meredith Bell

Before You Begin

The Decision to Quit (For Now)

People quit drinking for lots of reasons. I've learned from personal experience that a hard "rock bottom" situation isn't always necessary for many of us to think we've had enough. Maybe it's one bad night of embarrassing behavior that haunts your memory, or worse, a night you don't remember at all. It's possible that you've just gotten into a three-martini or one-bottle-of-wine habit that leaves you feeling debilitated rather than exhilarated. Maybe you have a medical issue that isn't compatible with drinking, or maybe you want to rid yourself of your unhealthy habits. Some people quit simply for financial reasons—and that makes sense, too.

It doesn't matter why you're taking this break. The point is not to pore over every slurred word, hellacious hangover or disastrous decision. The point of your seven days is to refocus your thoughts about your drinking while discovering healthier ways to spend your time.

There are a few simple steps that are required to get started on this journey. None of these changes are permanent—it's only seven days. You should be able to complete these first steps with relative ease. A little anxiety is to be expected. Work through it. Change is stressful for most people, but it's important to take a moment to acknowledge that you are embarking on a journey that may be frightening for you—and then do it anyway. Facing your fears is something that becomes easier once you've been sober for a while. A clear mind is an amazing anxiety reducer.

Here are the things you should do right away:

Buy, print or make a calendar that encompasses your seven days sober time frame. You don't have to put this in a public area, but do hang it somewhere you can see it. The calendar serves as a visual reminder not only of how much time you have left, but how much you have already accomplished. Mark every day you spend completely sober with an "X." It seems simple and hokey, but I find that scratching those "X" marks at the end of the day makes me feel like I have accomplished something.

Remove alcoholic beverages, mixers and other alcohol-related consumables from your home. When I did my first real seven days sober, I had recently left my husband and our massive wine cellar behind. The small apartment I lived in was alcohol free and I didn't go out and buy anything new. If you have a stash and can dump the booze then go for it.

Tell a friend or family member what you're doing. You don't have to tell them why, but letting someone else know your plan—and asking for their support—is a great way to stick to your guns. Choose wisely. Telling your most favorite drinking buddy that you're cooling your jets for seven days may result in a concerted effort to talk you out of it. Tell a long-distance relative, your pastor, a teacher or someone who doesn't have a vested interest in your continued drinking. An even better solution is to pick a friend to complete the seven days sober plan along with you. That way you can check in with each other and provide support when needed.

Come up with a reward. When you've been sober for the entire seven days, give yourself a little treat. I like to take myself to a spa, but you could treat yourself to a fancy meal, a trip, one million dollars—anything that works to keep you excited and engaged in this experience.

Look at your seven days as a gift, not a punishment. I was having a gossipy girls' lunch with a friend of mine who told me about the problems her husband was having adjusting to a major life change. He was bought out of a business that he helped create, and he was having a really difficult time figuring out what to do next. He spent a lot of time puttering around the house, and his drinking had taken a turn for the worse. As a person who worked in the alcohol industry since he was a teen, he had participated in his fair share of heavy drinking. Without the structure of full-time employment his drinking had taken on a different tone. The booze was harder, the nights were longer and the drinking started earlier. But what my friend was really focused on was that her husband needed to find some "real work "to snap him out of his downward spiral."

I suggested that he might need to take a few days off from drinking to pull himself together. A week or so to relax, I said. Maybe take a few walks, get a good night's sleep and, with newfound clarity, tackle the next phase of his life. I in no way suggested that he needed to quit for good, just for now. To get a grip.

Her response chilled me, and I think about it all the time when I get a little craving for a glass of wine. She said, "If he stopped drinking, wouldn't that just be *sad*?"

Sad? Taking a break from a substance you don't need—and that is clearly standing in the way of your forward progress—is sad? Taking a break from your nightly buzz to re-focus on the things in your life that you really want is *sad*? Looking at your life through clear eyes to create an actionable plan to meet your goals is *sad*? I guess it's sad if you view getting ripped and hungover as a reward for your hard work, a symbol of a life well lived or something you've earned. But let's get a little perspective. It's only a few days, after all.

It's not sad to say no to alcohol for a little while. What would be truly sad is if you kept drinking to run away from your problems rather than dealing with them. It would be sad if drinking stood in the way of building the dream life you deserve.

This week, I encourage you to embrace your seven days of sobriety with joy, enthusiasm and vigor. There is nothing sad about taking control of your life.

There's a wonderful quote in Allen Carr's book, *The Easy Way to Stop Drinking*. He says that after you complete his program you'll change your thought from "I don't *get* to drink anymore" to "I don't *have* to drink anymore." I love that sentiment, and will rephrase it here for our purposes: you don't have to drink for seven days. You can step away from an addictive substance that you know isn't healthy, that makes your thinking muddled and that depletes your energy. You simply don't have to do it. For seven days, you're *free*. And if you choose to see it as a gift you will be thoroughly rewarded with better sleep, more free time, an energetic outlook and the serenity that comes with knowing you're more in control of your life than ever before.

Schedule your seven days at a time when you can be successful. It's admirable that you'd want to take on a week of sobriety during your sister's wedding, right before graduation or as your family reunion approaches. I fully support that, especially if you believe that sobriety during these events will help you enjoy them more (it will). But I ask you to be realistic about your decision and to try your seven days when you know you can accomplish them. *Don't sabotage yourself.*

If you can, remove events where there will be drinking from your schedule. When I first started with seven days sober I eliminated after-work bar trips, weekend dinner parties and evenings out with the girls so I could take the sober life for a test drive. It was easier for me. However, if you find that this is impossible, I have shared some tips on Day Six on how to sail through these events soberly.

Ask for medical help if you need it. If you are experiencing serious detoxification issues such as shakes, sweats, hallucinations or physical pain, I urge you to see a doctor immediately. **I will repeat: this is not something to be taken lightly—people die from alcohol withdrawal.** This guide—savvy as it may be—is not designed to provide the qualified medical assistance you need for a severe detoxification. You and your doctor should decide how you should proceed with any treatment.

Keep a journal if you'd like, or at least be prepared to spend some time on the questions posed for each day. At the end of each day's lesson there are some questions and ideas that you're encouraged to ponder. I've tried to provide some queries that would get you thinking about your drinking in ways you may not have up to this point. The idea is not to judge you or put you on the spot in any way, only to allow you to get an assessment of how you're really feeling about the role alcohol plays in your life.

Ignore Your Inner Voice

Like a dear friend whom you love but who gets you in trouble with their constant need for rowdy shenanigans, your inner voice is going to work like hell to get you off track. It's going to say things like:

"You haven't had a drink for two days! Congratulations. Problem solved. Let's celebrate with a glass of wine."

"What's just one? You can have one drink tonight—that's not really considered 'drinking.' Just one. A small one. And then you can stop."

"You had a difficult day. Your boss is an asshole, your mom's mean, the kids are driving you crazy. You can't get through this without a drink."

Ignore! Ignore! Ignore! Do not pay any attention whatsoever to your inner voice. You can't trust it right now. When it gets going, simply explain to it that you have made a decision not to drink this week so it needs to shut up. And then ignore it some more. Your inner voice cannot be trusted.

This is Not the Week for Major Life Changes

Taking a break from drinking is enough for now. The idea is to pause, reflect and renew so that you can approach your relationship with alcohol with a better understanding of its role in your decisions, your health, your happiness and every other aspect of your life. I caution you against using your newfound energy to make a clean sweep of everything that's not working for you.

I strongly recommend against the following actions during your seven days sober:

Breaking up with a spouse or partner

Moving

Quitting your job

Starting a new job

Finally telling your family/mother/father/best friends what you REALLY think of them

Getting married

Starting or quitting school

Starting a new hobby

Starting a new romantic relationship

Changing your haircut or hair color

Getting a tattoo

Getting a pet

You might suspect that these major life changes would make it difficult for you to stay sober, and that's actually true. But that's not why I'm cautioning you against it. I believe that this program is most effective when you are living your life *just as it is now*. It's the only way to discover your true relationship with alcohol, not the relationship you have with alcohol when major parts of your life are completely new, fresh and different. If you're simultaneously experiencing a major shift, you're not going to get an accurate picture of your drinking habits and beliefs. Keep things the same this week to see what you learn.

However, if you recently completed some of these major changes and are trying seven days sober as an addition to a positive life change, that's terrific. And if you make the decision to take on any of these things when you're done, then you know you made the decision with mental acuity and an attitude uninfluenced by mood altering chemicals.

My First Time Quitting

My first real attempt at long-term sobriety wasn't my choice. Oh, I knew that I needed to quit, and I had gone one or two days without drinking before, but I never honestly considered quitting for good. What was different this time was that I was seeing a therapist to help me with the depression I felt throughout my marriage, and my sadness that the marriage was ending. We were successfully addressing many of the emotional problems I had been struggling with, and I found the process to be incredibly rewarding. Even though it was painful, I was developing insight into my condition and building trust with my therapist, who I thought was a very competent, intelligent and thoughtful partner.

I was about 12 weeks in to weekly, sometimes twice-weekly, sessions. That's when she told me she would not work with me anymore unless I quit drinking.

She claimed that we would be unable to continue with any of this work unless I got the alcohol completely out of my system and learned to deal with life soberly.

To say this came as a shock is a massive understatement. I was doing so well! I was really getting somewhere! Did she really think I needed to quit drinking? How could this be if I was feeling so much better?

Her firm answer was that she would terminate our working relationship if I did not commit to attending AA meetings.

I drove home and collapsed on my floor, where I sobbed myself to sleep.

The next day, she took me to my first AA meeting. I remained sober for nearly two years.

Day One:

Begin at the Beginning

Congratulations! You are taking the first step toward a better understanding of the role drinking plays in your life. This is your time to press the reset button, clear the cache and face the reality of your drinking head on. This is not a punishment or a reproach in any way. In fact, this seven day sober time out is a small gift you're giving yourself—a slight nudge toward living a more fulfilling life—with or without alcohol.

On this first day you're going to spend time preparing your mindset for the rest of the week. I'm going to explore the expectations and emotions you may experience and offer some advice on how to best handle each one. I've experienced everything on these pages and can tell you with certainty that, although you may be very uncomfortable at times, you will be very glad that you stuck with it at the end. Just stick with it!

There Are No Epiphanies

Throughout all of my years of drinking I kept waiting for that "movie moment" where a certain event, action or decision would result in complete clarity. A moment where my next steps would be illuminated in glorious golden light. A moment that would instantly snap me into some sort of resolve I hadn't been able to muster on my own.

We see this magic moment all the time in films and on TV. The hero witnesses something life changing and never again cheats on his wife, takes another drink, steals money from orphans, beats his kids… Or the epiphany instantly fills him with motivation to pen his novel, train for that marathon, apply to night school or any number of other things that would be life changing in a positive way.

If you've been waiting for the epiphany that makes quitting drinking absolutely effortless, stop right now. It's not coming. There are no epiphanies. Epiphanies are made up by screenwriters to make their storylines fit into 90-minute blocks of time. No one is interested in a movie that shows the actual minute-by-minute effort that goes into making true and lasting change.

Real change happens day-by-day, hour-by-hour and minute-by-minute. True accomplishment is measured in small, simple decisions. Will I head to the bar with my friends this afternoon or will I go for a hike? Will I flip through the channels before I go to bed or will I spend an hour working on my book? Will I drive to McDonald's or to the gym? Will I mix one more cocktail or will I put myself to bed?

There are no epiphanies. If you can get your head around this one life lesson, your ability to make better decisions will increase with practice in every single moment. Stop waiting for the sky to open up, and for flashes of brilliant light to make your life work. That's not coming. But know that your opportunity to make better decisions is happening right now, in this moment, always in this moment.

Emotions May Run High This Week

Although I am a big believer in the ultimate positive outcome of taking a break from drinking, I am not immune to the emotions that come along with abstaining from alcohol.

Here are some of the things you may feel during your seven days. I ask you to remember that these feelings are just feelings. They are not permanent. The more you sit with them, the less overwhelming they will become.

Euphoria

At some point you may be so overtaken with energy that you feel you can accomplish anything. This is a wonderful feeling, but I caution you to approach it like you would any of your more "negative" responses. Exercise, take a brisk walk or tackle some of the projects at the end of the book when you're feeling this way. Enjoy euphoria while you can, but if it goes away don't beat yourself up about it. Moving through euphoria and back again is indicative of your emotions stabilizing. You've been influencing your emotional state with alcohol up to this point so it makes sense that you're going to have some highs and lows that are accustomed to being balanced with booze. Take a breath, enjoy the high energy and relax.

Anxiety

I have a lot of personal experience with anxiety. I'm anxious when I drink and I'm anxious when I don't drink. If you're feeling anxious about how you're going to get through the next seven days, that's completely understandable. It's likely that you've been using alcohol as your main coping mechanism, and without something to replace it, you're going to feel like you're on a high wire without a net. This is the addiction to the alcohol and the alcohol-based routine talking.

Anxiety is the normal condition of life. Without healthy anxiety we wouldn't show up to work on time, wear our seatbelts or lock our doors at night. When anxiety comes knocking, call it out for what it is: a distraction from your task at hand. And remember, the best way to handle anxiety is to breathe deeply—not take a drink.

Boredom

If you're accustomed to highlighting your day with an alcoholic beverage, it's possible that you will not know what to do with your free time. I drank every single day for about ten years, and when I finally decided to give it a rest I lacked the imagination to see what I would possibly do instead. I would get home by six, pour myself a tall glass of chardonnay and spend the evening chatting on the phone, watching reality TV and drinking. Would I exercise? Nope. Go for a walk? Never. Create something? Nah-uh. For the first few days after I quit I sat on the couch and chewed my fingernails. Then I cleaned. Then, I got some courage and looked for better ways to spend my time.

Over time, I found that the things I enjoyed doing were no longer compatible with drinking. I discovered that I love to hike, practice yoga and write. I enjoy riding my bike, working in my garden and organizing my finances. You might find that you like to do other things with your time, but until you open up that space in your life and let in some boredom, you may not ever be motivated to find anything to do other than drink.

Embrace boredom! If the boredom is overwhelming, I invite you to check out the Special Section at the end of the book. It's filled with clever ways to spend your non-drinking time and the resources to help you on your way.

Anger

"Everyone around me drinks, so why am I the one who has to quit?"

"Why can't I be allowed to have a few drinks and not feel like crap the next day?"

"This is so stupid. Drinking is a part of my life and it's going to be impossible for me to quit."

Sound familiar? This is the anger talking, and it's going to be loud. I was so angry and bitter when I was first told that I had a drinking problem that I became unbearable to be around. I didn't get why I had to focus on my drinking while everyone else I knew was off blissfully imbibing whatever it is they wanted, whenever they wanted, and nobody was getting on their case about it.

I moved through the anger—the snapping at people, the lack of patience with absolutely everything—without a drink. When I got to the other side I became aware that my anger was really my fear talking. *I was afraid that I couldn't do it.* I was terrified that I couldn't quit drinking even if I wanted to. And I put this wall of anger up to justify why I shouldn't try.

I don't really know how other people's drinking affects them. Maybe they do sail through a bottle of wine a night and wake up the next morning refreshed and ready to take on the day. Who knows? But that wasn't my experience. Mine was one of blackouts, inappropriate behavior, vomiting and exhaustion. So I could be mad about that, and I was. I was furious. But I soon realized that if I channeled my anger into something positive, I stopped feeling mad and started feeling energized about my new life direction. Let others keep drinking if they want. But try to keep it in perspective. Quitting drinking for seven days isn't anything to be all that angry about when you consider all the positive things you're getting back.

Sadness

For many drinkers, including myself, saying goodbye to alcohol feels like a death. In many ways it is. If you're really being honest about a drinking problem at some point you will have to face that a part of you is going to leave and never come back. Be sad, but don't worry. The part of you that you're grieving for is your unhealthy part—the sick part of you that feels that it needs a chemical booster to get through the day. In Allen Carr's *The Easy Way to Control Alcohol*, he makes a brilliant point that the human body has everything it needs to manage its own stress. We don't need outside chemicals. The unhealthy part of you has tricked you into thinking that you need alcohol to function. You don't.

But that doesn't mean that you won't mourn the loss of this crutch. I saw a comedian once—I wish I could remember his name because I would love to offer the credit here—who said that quitting drinking was much harder for him than quitting smoking. When asked why, he responded, "You don't ever sit around with your friends and say, 'Remember that time we bought a pack of cigarettes and stayed up all night talking?'" The alcohol has been part of your friendships, part of your mealtime rituals and part of your nightly unwind routine. You may feel like you're losing a friend.

There are two things to remember when the sadness washes over you. 1) You've only committed at this point to seven days. Your friend went on a vacation. 2) If you do decide to say goodbye forever at the end of this journey, you're saying goodbye to a friend who stole your money, stole your time, brought unnecessary drama and anxiety to your life and who continually zapped your energy. Feel sad, but see the sadness as a temporary blip. The real joy awaits you around the corner.

Regret

The major stumbling block in my sobriety is the overwhelming feeling of regret. Not only did I screw up relationships, jobs and opportunities with my drinking, but I also robbed myself of my most potentially productive years. There are some things that passed me by that now, because of my age, I'll never be able to do again. There are also some people to whom, because of my carelessness, I'll never be able to speak again. There were some great jobs that I should have had that I didn't take because I was too focused on my drinking.

Case in point: After I had been in the wine industry for a number of years, I was feeling ready for a change. I applied for and got an interview with a well-respected national tea company. This was an entrepreneurial group with an exciting philosophy, not only about business, but also about life and simple pleasures. Despite the fact that I showed up to one of my interviews with a massive hangover, I was offered the job and I took it. I gave two weeks' notice at my other job and celebrated a few days of "short-timer's syndrome"—that joyful condition experienced by those who are about to leave or change jobs.

I drank like a rock star every night, and drove to my current job hungover every morning. About a week into this all-out revelry, I got worried. I was a heavy drinker who stayed up late every night with my best friend, chardonnay. Every morning was an endless set of machinations designed to hoist me out of hangover hell. But in the wine business, this behavior was *overlooked*. I could get away with being sluggish simply because most other people at my office were in the same listing boat.

I worried that these tea drinkers might not be so supportive. They may expect me to hit the ground running at 8 a.m.

sharp instead of lingering around the soda machine until noon. They may not shrug it off if I showed up a few minutes late because I couldn't get my shit together in the morning. They may not find a high-functioning alcoholic funny, cute or "one of us."

After a few days of handwringing, I called my new boss and told him I wasn't going to take the job. I didn't tell him why, but I knew in that moment that I was cementing my future as a heavy drinker. I was in full-blown addiction and I would have done anything, even sabotage my career, to keep feeding the beast. I found a new job in the wine industry, and I kept up my old drinking pattern for several more years because I could hide it in plain sight.

I still see ads for the tea company, and I buy their wonderful products all the time now that I no longer buy wine! But I always wonder what might have been if I had taken that job and gotten sober sooner.

We have all done regretful things to preserve our drinking. You may regret the way you talked to your kids when they found your stash. You may regret driving home from the bar because you couldn't admit you needed a cab. You may regret never having children because you didn't think you could quit drinking for nine whole months. You are not alone in regret.

To deal with regret I have to acknowledge the feeling and be honest with myself that yes, this did happen and, yes, it is my fault. But then I spend a few minutes thinking about all the things in my life for which I am a currently very grateful—wonderful things that may not have happened if I didn't also make some bad decisions along the way.

Loneliness

Drinking is a social activity. For many of us it's our main social activity. We gather our buddies after work and rev up the blender or pop the corks. We hang out at all-day barbecues. We plan girls' nights or guys' nights with the sole mission of getting ripped.

If you've decided to forego some of these activities this week, you might feel lonely. If you go to these activities and are the only one not drinking, you still might feel lonely.

Loneliness is a tough emotion to tackle because sometimes it's the by-product of something else. For example, how many times have you been in a room full of people and still felt lonely? How many times have you been completely alone and not felt lonely at all?

Loneliness can be a manifestation of the sadness or a depression we feel from being unable to really connect with people. Oprah Winfrey once said something that really resonated with me. She said, "All people want to be *seen*."

In my own drinking journey, the crux off all of my sadness, anxiety and loneliness came from my desire to be truly seen. I used alcohol to connect with people, but it was artificial. I was as lonely as before, only now I was also throwing up in my host's backyard and passing out on his coffee table.

Look at your loneliness to see where it really comes from. Do you miss the drinking or are you longing for a real, intimate connection based in reality? Reflect on this feeling of separateness to see if it's true—are you really alone? Or are you afraid to share the deeper part of yourself? Are you covering up your true self with alcohol?

Bad Sleep

This isn't really an emotion, but when your sleep patterns get out of whack it can send you into an emotional tailspin. If you drink every day your brain relies on the relaxing effects of alcohol to help you drift off. When you remove the sedative your brain simply might not know how to wind down.

Don't worry. This is an extremely common side effect of quitting drinking, and it will only last a few days. My best advice is to not panic—use the time while you're awake to take on some of the activities at the end of the book. The Japanese have a lovely belief that when the mind refuses to sleep, it's because there is a problem it wants to be working on. (This philosophy has completely revolutionized my thoughts on insomnia, in a good way). Embrace your insomnia and use the time to your advantage. Finish up that work project or watch a movie. It may be a bit frazzling, but it will pass. And when it does, the deep, satisfying sleep you enjoy while sober will surprise you.

Satisfaction

Satisfaction is guaranteed on a seven-day sober journey. If you can weather seven days without a drink, and decide once and for all whether you want to continue, I promise you'll feel proud of yourself, more in control and healthier than ever before. You'll be clear-headed enough to take on the next phase.

Whether you're moving toward moderation or absolute abstinence, you know that you came to your decision with your best self. Plus, along the way you may have tackled some of the projects at the end of the book. Each one is designed to help un-muddy those waters by moving your body, managing your daily life and getting rid of all the things you don't need. If you've done all of that and completed seven days sober, congratulations! You're on your way to managing your drinking and not having it manage you.

Peace

You've completed seven days sober. You've eaten nutritious meals, and maybe you've seen your doctor and gotten useful health information. You've slept better than you have in years and taken a few brisk walks. You've sat quietly with uncomfortable feelings. Maybe you've been a conspicuous non-drinker at a drinking event. You've made some concrete decisions about how you are going to proceed with your life. What is that strange serenity that's come over you? That's what we call *peace.*

Peace might be the most uncomfortable feeling of all. For those of us with even the slightest hint of self-destructive behavior, a peaceful feeling is enough to send us straight for the bottle. *"I'm feeling so good, I think I'll have a drink to celebrate."*

I discovered early on in my sobriety attempts that I often mistake relaxation for sadness. I had gotten so accustomed to being wound up by alcohol and all the drama that came with it, that when the feelings of peace finally washed over me I thought I was depressed.

Don't fall into this trap. If you're feeling peaceful you've earned it. Don't take it for granted and don't use it as an excuse to fall off your wagon. Enjoy the little Mona Lisa smile that's crept to your lips. Revel in the mellow feeling in your chest. For once, just *be.*

That's a pretty good overview of some of the major feelings you may have this week. Good or bad, each one has its pitfalls, so stay focused. Remember: the only way out is through. You cannot process an emotion in a healthy way by running from it. If you feel anything strongly this week—ranging from happy to sad and all the highs and lows in between—feel the emotion, let it wash over you, sit with it and then release it.

Questions to Consider:

Why did you decide to take a break from drinking?

What was your first drinking experience like?

What do you hope to accomplish during this week off from drinking?

Have you been waiting for an epiphany to make it easier for you to stop drinking?

Are you feeling any negative emotions about your decision? What about positive emotions?

What is your inner voice saying to you today? Are you able to ignore it?

Day Two:

Sobriety Toolbox

It's a drinker's world out there. You can't always avoid social situations where people are drinking, but you can take control of your own drinking while you're there. I've discovered a few things in my own sobriety that will make it easier for you to tackle situations where you may be tempted to drink.

How to Not be Awkward When You Decide Not to Drink

I have a theory that situations are only as awkward as we allow them to be. You can't control how someone else responds to your decision not to drink so it's really up to you how awkward you want to feel about it. You've made a decision for your health and well-being. You want to take a break from drinking, whether it's this week, tonight or forever—and that's all. You're not condemning anyone else's choice to drink. You're not claiming that you're somehow better than them. YOU have no reason to feel awkward, so my advice to you is… Don't feel awkward. Besides, you'll feel a lot less awkward later when you realize you left a social event without having to worry about what embarrassing thing you said to someone.

Other people may feel awkward in your presence and this can result in a few reactions:

- Their behavior will be demonstrably uncomfortable
- They will avoid you
- They will make jokes, usually at your expense

- They will try to convince you to drink with them

There are only a few ways for you to respond if you aren't prepared:

- You can be demonstrably uncomfortable (not recommended)
- You can avoid others (not recommended)
- You can make jokes at your expense (not recommended)
- You can drink with them and get it over with (not recommended)

Or, you can create an action plan that doesn't involve you reacting to their reaction at all.

Here are some strategies to try:

Set a time that you will leave the event, and stick to it. Sometimes planning a quick drop-by is adequate to help you not only avoid cravings, but to also alleviate the stress of needing to have a reason why you're not drinking. If you're in and out fast enough you'll be able to stick to your decision not to drink without attracting too much attention. This plan is not a long-term solution. It's going to be pretty impossible for you to just "pop in" to social events indefinitely. But for now—while you're still new at being sober at parties—there's no reason why you can't keep it short. Think of it this way: most people at the party will be getting tipsy so they won't really be focused on what you're doing anyway.

Hold a glass filled with water or soda to lessen the chances that someone will offer you a refill of an alcoholic beverage. I know a famous sommelier who is also a raging alcoholic (this is much more common than you might think). His life's work revolves around recommending wines, so it's very difficult for him to explain why he's not drinking. My friend's strategy is to fill a wine glass with water and keep it full. That way he can avoid the inevitable refill requests, and the presence of a wine glass in his hand puts people at ease. Plus, lots of people drink water between their alcoholic drinks, so having a glass full of water is in no way unusual. This seems like a lot of work, I know, but it's up to us to take charge of the situation.

Develop a few "no thank you" phrases to help you turn down a drink. If you're known for being a drinker, this might be one of the most difficult things you'll face in a social situation. For years, I couldn't say anything that didn't draw attention to the fact I wasn't drinking. "YOU'RE not drinking?" people would say, incredulous. "Are you pregnant?" (SO many times I had to explain that I'm not pregnant...) Saying "no thanks," won't cut it for those of us with a reputation. So here are some of the things I say:

"I have to be somewhere early tomorrow and if I start now, you know I won't stop!"

"I don't want to drink and drive tonight. But I'll be more than happy to drive your drunk ass home if you need it."

"My trainer says no drinking during the week[end]. It's tough, but she really wants me to meet my goal weight, and cutting out alcohol is helping."

Remember, even if you tell a mini white lie to diffuse the situation, that's ok. It is no one else's business whether you drink or not, so whatever you have to do to get the spotlight off of you is just fine.

Also, if you're really determined, you can always remind yourself that "no" is a complete sentence.

Don't touch any alcohol. If you don't have it in your fist, you can't get it to your lips. Don't go to the cooler to get your friend a beer. Don't pass the winc bottle to the person next to you. Don't fetch refills. Don't touch it no matter what. I like to make a game of this, akin to not stepping on cracks in the sidewalk.

Not drinking for an hour, a day, a week, a month or a year is a choice for your health and happiness. Think of it this way: if you told your friends that you were training for a marathon, they would applaud your choice as healthy, ambitious and impressive. I don't know why it has to be this way, but I doubt they will respond to your choice to quit drinking with the same enthusiasm. I'm asking you right now to be your own cheerleader. You know you are doing something as important as training for a marathon so congratulate yourself. And stick to your guns. You'll be so glad you did.

Remember: You Will Never Regret Not Drinking

When was the last time you woke up in the morning and wished you'd had *one more drink* the night before?

Let me flip that around: when was the last time you woke up in the morning and wished you hadn't had a drink at all?

I have never, in any time of sobriety, regretted not taking a drink. In fact, I have usually felt proud of myself, well rested, in control and free from anxiety. If I was the only one in the room not drinking, I may have felt a little out of place at the time (or gotten a little antsy when the chardonnay emerged from the fridge). But nothing, I mean *nothing* in my life is more satisfying at this point than knowing that I didn't do or say anything regrettable, that I didn't go home with someone I hardly know, that my clothes stayed on and that I am hangover free. And the only way I can guarantee that I feel that way is if I don't drink.

I have never once regretted not drinking. Say this to yourself, and you'll get through anything.

Some Slogans to Keep You Sane

When getting through without a drink feels more difficult than it should, I like to repeat a few slogans to myself. Having go-to phrases at the ready calms me down, and I instantly find perspective. Some of my favorites are from AA; others are my own. Some of these you've already read scattered throughout the book.

Caution: these are hokey. But they work, and I am not ashamed to admit it!

Less drama. More laundry.

I'm sick and tired of being sick and tired.

My life works better when I'm not drinking.

Try being sober for a few days, and if you don't like it we will gladly refund your misery.

I don't have to refuse all alcoholic drinks, just the first one.

HALT: Don't get too hungry, angry, lonely or tired.

Progress, not perfection.

"No" is a complete sentence.

Expectations are premeditated resentments.

Measure yourself by your best moments, not your worst.

I've had enough.

If you think you're an alcoholic, you probably are.

Most things worth doing are done alone.

I have never regretted not drinking.

I have never wished that I had "just one more" the night before.

You will always live up to your own expectations.

Questions to Consider:

Have you ever attended an event where alcohol is served and not had a drink? How did you feel?

How are your cravings so far? How are you managing them?

What has been the most difficult part so far?

How is your energy level today? How is your sleep?

Have you ever regretted not taking a drink?

Do you have any slogans of your own that contribute to your own health and well-being?

Day Three:

Friends and Family

Your friends and family aren't guaranteed to get it when and if you tell them you're taking a break from drinking. In fact, nearly everyone I told tried to talk me out of quitting for ANY length of time.

It's your life, it's your decision and, at this point, it's just SEVEN DAYS. In today's reading, we're going to explore the possible reactions you'll face and how to respond.

When Your Friends Freak Out

When I first looked in the mirror and could no longer run away from the fact that I had developed an abusive relationship with alcohol, one of the first things I did was turn to my friends and my then-husband to get their support. I wanted to quit, and who better to help than the people with whom I previously gotten plastered?

That never panned out. In fact, my friends and husband were, if not entirely dismissive, they were openly hostile.

The reactions ranged from "You don't have a drinking problem…" (said in the same disbelieving tone someone would use to say, "You never bobsledded in the Olympics…"), to "Just because you're not drinking anymore doesn't mean that my guests won't." (This last one came after my first few AA meetings when I discovered soon-to-be ex-husband installing a brand new wine bar in our home.)

One therapist suggested that maybe it wasn't my drinking that's the problem but "how I *feel* about" my drinking is the problem.

Let's explore these reactions.

"You don't have a drinking problem."

If your friends drink as much or more than you do this is a reaction you're definitely going to get. My rule on this is that if you think you have a problem, you do. If you don't think you have a problem, but you think you could be headed in that direction, own that and honor it. Take control of it and do something about it.

When my friends reacted this way, I was relieved at first. I interpreted this as a validation that I didn't act as crazy as I thought I did. But I couldn't lie to *myself.* I knew that after a heavy night of drinking I could continue to feel sick for days. I knew that if I didn't have at least three glasses of wine before bed I would wake up with night sweats. I was aware that I frequently chose not to accompany my husband on business trips because I preferred to be in the house drinking alone. That hilarious thing that happened at the party? I have no recollection of it because I was a blackout drinker.

Your friends are absolutely unqualified to make this assessment for you. Only you know what's really going on.

"Just because you're not drinking anymore doesn't mean that [I, our guests, our friends] won't drink anymore."

This is true. If you decide to continue abstaining from alcohol you can't expect anyone else to join you on this journey. But it's also an openly hostile response—or that's how I took it. If someone very close to you is unwilling to support your choice for better health and a clear mind, then perhaps you need to look at the relationship in a different light.

Acquaintances, work colleagues and other not-so-close friends and family members should not be expected to stop drinking because you did. But if you come home to find your best friend, roommate, parents or life partner installing a new wine bar, joining a new wine club or mixing up a new cocktail while you're on this journey, you may need to spend some time thinking about the role drinking plays in your relationships.

"It's not the drinking, it's how you *feel* about your drinking that's the problem."

This is by far the weirdest response I ever encountered. It's possible that the people who said this were trying to make me feel less ashamed about my drinking. I suppose that this is another way to say that they didn't think I had a drinking problem. And it's also possible that it's one of those things people say when they're less concerned about your well-being and more concerned with losing their drinking buddy.

It's sort of absurd, and possibly self-serving, to advise someone to just change the way they feel about drinking when it's clear they want to quit. It's like saying your pneumonia isn't the problem, it's how you feel about having pneumonia is the problem.

I think this response comes from the fact that drinking alcohol is addictive. Most people who drink alcohol on a daily basis are addicted to it physically, emotionally and spiritually. Anyone who says that how you "feel" about your drinking is the problem has possibly looked at themselves in the mirror, bleary-eyed from a night of boozing, and decided in that moment that they are going to be ok with this. Accepting a life of drunken disconnection is easier than making a change. It's also, in many ways, easier than forging real relationships, achieving goals and finding more wholesome ways to spend your time.

If you have a problem with your drinking, if you *feel* that you are out of control, close to being out of control or want to take a break from the dizziness, hangovers, lost keys, sluggish workdays, poor sleep and low energy, you should explore those feelings.

So, yes. How I *felt* about my drinking was the problem. I *felt* that it was ruining my life. I was right.

Why Some People Will Try to Talk You Out of It

People are protective of their drinking. When their drinking buddies quit they get defensive. In my heavy drinking days I made fun of people who didn't drink. Why is it that when we're drinking we're so put out by people who don't choose to drink? Why does the non-drinker make the drinker feel self-conscious, defensive and hostile?

Maybe it's because somewhere in the drinking unconscious we know that what we're doing is wrong. And by "wrong" I don't mean morally wrong—I personally don't believe that drinking is a moral issue whatsoever. Some of the activities we allow ourselves to engage in while drinking may cross the line into morals, but the actual act of putting booze into our face has no good or bad value other than what we attach to it.

But I do think our spirit somehow responds negatively to the choice to imbibe a chemical that takes us out of our experience. Alcohol blurs our responses, dulls our emotions and damages our ability to make good decisions. I think those defensive responses might come from a place within us that wishes it could break free of the desire to drink and instead embrace a more complete life experience.

I also still experience moments with friends who drink who are adamant that they could "never" quit, or prattle on about why their drinking habit doesn't merit quitting. (Usually it's something along the lines of, *"I know how to pace myself."* To which I always respond, *"That sounds like a lot of work."*)

When people make a change in their lives like quitting drinking, taking up exercise or changing their diet, others interpret this as a criticism of their own choices. I'm telling you now that my decision to quit drinking, to eat less meat and to exercise daily has nothing to do with you or anyone else. I am not trying to change anyone or convert any other human to my beliefs (although I do hope this book helps people find insight into a situation that's vexing them).

When people come after you with a defensive posture they are trying to make *your* decision about *them*. Remind them that it's your own personal choice and that they don't need to change because you did. Then take a deep breath and remind yourself that, likewise, their reaction has nothing to do with you.

Schadenfreude

If you're not familiar with this term, I encourage you to take a few moments to understand the effect it's going to have on your journey. *Schadenfreude* is the feeling of happiness at someone else's misfortune. It's the mechanism we use to feel better about ourselves when someone else is struggling. It comes from our own fear of the same mishap occurring in our own lives, coupled with the belief that we're so superior that nothing like that can happen to us.

If you're at all open about diminishing the amount you drink or—heavens forbid—you admit to anyone that you think you have a problem, your drinking friends are going to engage in hearty doses of schadenfreude, probably behind your back, because they are trying to defend their own drinking.

Is it because they are so addicted to alcohol themselves that they can't make it the drink's fault? They will convince themselves that this has to be some failing in you, some moral error, some character flaw of yours and *yours alone* because they don't want to give up their own addiction.

But the problem isn't you. It's the alcohol. I can't stress this enough: alcohol is powerfully addictive. When people try to break free, others who continue to drink can be very rattled. They have to make it the non-drinker's fault. *What's wrong with them can't possibly be wrong with me, right?* That's an addiction talking.

This is going to hurt. The reason I bring it up here is because I need to remind you that you haven't done anything wrong. You are addicted to a chemical that is created with the sole purpose of making you addicted. The creators of the alcohol have done their job. It's not your fault. You can be proud that you're getting to the bottom of the problem that's been plaguing you. And when you conquer it, you can feel good about being armed with the tools that are going to get you off the barstool and back into your life.

When Support is Offered, Take It

Some of your friends and family may respond to your seven-day break with a phrase like, "Finally..." or "We're so glad to hear it." These are the folks who have seen your drinking take a turn for the worse but were afraid to say something. If you decide to share your seven-day sober journey—and you get this response—these concerned friends will offer help. Take them up on it.

Ask them to go for a walk, play a game or go to a movie. If they are moderate drinkers or completely sober, pick their brains about the kinds of things they do instead of drinking, and ask to come along. When I stopped drinking (all THREE times) I was continually shocked—and that's not an overstatement—to discover all the things people did instead of drinking. I was flabbergasted that you could go out to dinner on a Friday and *drink sparkling water because you wanted to get up early to go hiking.* I mean, *for reals*? This had literally never occurred to me.

I latched on to people with healthier habits and found that there is a whole wide world of people, even in wine country, who embrace a life of sobriety, mental acuity, physical activity and peace of mind. When I asked for support from the right people, people who were newly sober or people who never had more than two drinks a week, my world changed in ways that I could not have possibly predicted.

You Can Keep Your Seven Days to Yourself

Although I recommended telling someone earlier in the book, you don't have to. This is your private journey. You can stay home every night and read, watch TV and knit to get through your seven days. You can leave town and stay in a hotel, at a resort or housesit for seven days. You can do this as quietly as you choose. It is no one's business but your own, and if you decide to keep it to yourself that is a fine decision.

If you do decide to go this completely alone, be your own best friend. I beat myself up about how I used to behave when I was actively drinking. I still feel regret and shame for the nasty gossip I spread, the hurtful things I said about my friends and family and the important events that I missed.

Do not slip into this kind of thinking. If you're feeling ashamed, embarrassed, guilty or sad, talk to yourself like you would talk to a friend. Would you continue to lambast him for the mistakes he's made? Or would you tell him that the past is the past, and that he can make positive changes in the future, starting right now? Would you help him spiral down further into depression by calling him names, or would you comfort and soothe his battered spirit with uplifting words and gentle humor?

Be careful how you talk to yourself. Be supportive of your bruised ego and be gentle with the language you use with yourself right now. You're doing a good thing. And tomorrow is always another opportunity to make things right.

My Terrible Inner Critic

I may have suffered blackouts, memory loss and selective amnesia throughout my darkest years of drinking, but in sobriety I have no trouble recalling the awful things I did.

My inner critic is mean. It uses words like "stupid," "ridiculous," and "failure" to describe my personality. It reminds me that even though I have control of this now, I am a bad, worthless, lazy, drunk person who did awful things and wasted several years of my life. I ruined relationships and put others in harm's way on more occasions than I can count. The images of my crazy, out-of-control behavior flash through my mind like images in a slide show, haunting me with hundreds of painful recollections.

It's easy for me to get swept up in these feelings of guilt and remorse. I feel them physically, like a gut punch. But when I sense these feelings coming on, I acknowledge them, breathe deeply, experience them completely and then let them go. I can't fix the past, but I can use these negative feelings in a positive way. I work hard to transform my negative emotions into positive actions. When I am overwhelmed by my inner critic, I take a walk, I make food for someone else or I work on a creative project that has a positive message. I have to acknowledge these feelings and behaviors in order to recover from them, but I don't have to wallow in them—and neither do you.

Questions to Consider:

What reactions have you had in the past to others who don't drink or have quit drinking?

Do you worry that if you quit drinking others will assume you have a drinking problem? Would that be difficult for you?

Have you faced any opposition to your plan to quit drinking for a while? How did you react? Were you comfortable with your reaction or do you want to explore it further?

How are you sleeping? Do you have more energy?

Are you getting a sense of what it would be like to stay sober? Does sobriety still interest you?

Day Four:

What's Behind the Curtain?

Day Four is the perfect opportunity to identify the driving factors behind your drinking. It's a long-accepted belief that alcohol is a rite of passage, a gateway into adulthood and a reason to sit at the big table. This philosophy has been hammered into us by society through movies, TV, popular songs and alcohol advertising.

We've all been influenced by the societal pressure to drink (and to think drinking is wonderful and necessary), but on this day I'd like you to also consider your own mythos around drinking. I'm going to share my theory on "The Machine" that drives us to drink, and some of the falsehoods that have been perpetuated throughout history.

The Machine

I love talking to other ex-drinkers because, even though our backgrounds, reasons for drinking and reasons for quitting are often completely different, we nearly always share the same little quirks, habits and ways of thinking about drinking. I call this "The Machine." The Machine is comprised of those gears in your mind that are continually driving you toward drinking, grinding out thoughts about drinking and creating obsessive behaviors around alcohol. In active, abusive drinkers, The Machine is running on high gear 24 hours a day.

You've got The Machine if you've ever:

> Planned your evening's drinking while you're taking your morning shower, going for your morning run, or driving to work

Joined a gym or worked out for the express purpose of sweating alcohol out so you could drink more later

Worried, when sitting down to dinner or entering an event, that there wouldn't be enough alcohol to go around

Gotten anxious when you realized that there was no more booze in the house, at the party or at the dinner table

Brought your own stash to an event where you thought there might not be enough alcohol

Poured glasses of alcoholic beverages for yourself and others with precise levels to ensure that you got your fair share

Hurried home after a sports practice, rehearsal or a regular workday because you couldn't wait another minute to have a drink

Thought you may have a drinking problem but quickly shushed yourself because "you're not as bad" as someone you know, saw on TV or heard about

Hidden alcohol anywhere in your house, in your car, in someone else's house, in your yard, in your desk or behind the bed

Hidden your empty bottles or refused to put them in the recycling because you were afraid of what the neighbors might think

Taught yourself where all the most likely DUI checkpoints are in your hometown and learned to avoid them, even when sober

Used the phrase: "I don't know why I'm so drunk, I only had two glasses." (*Two glasses seems to be the go-to lie for every alcoholic I've met. In drunk math, two equals six...*)

Said to yourself: "What's one more? It's only [insert time here]. I'll be fine in the morning."

Awakened with a hangover and immediately called the host of the party or a friend to see if you should apologize for your behavior. You know you were drunk and embarrassing, but you want them to say, "I don't know what you're talking about. You were fine." You don't believe them, but it makes you feel better anyway.

Injured yourself while drinking and blamed it on "being clumsy"

Searched the web for hangover remedies

Looked at your bad skin and blamed it on a poor diet or lack of sleep

Bought wristbands, nose strips, neti pots, special vitamins or any other medical devices for the sole purpose of getting you through a hangover

Told yourself you'll never drink again in the morning, and then you're drinking again by the evening because you feel better

In my drinking days The Machine ran me ragged. It was exhausting to keep my eye on the level of the wine bottle at every single dinner I attended (and there were a lot!). It was embarrassing to always be the one to open or order the next bottle. I had to drive out of my way on several occasions to avoid getting tapped by the police. My finances took a hit, too. The Machine needed to be fed! My wine habit on a good day was at least $20. On "fancier" days where I chose a "special" bottle or I was "celebrating," it wouldn't faze me to drop $100 or more on booze.

If The Machine is running your life, I encourage you to look at this week as a break from the constant spinning. I've broken away from my Machine, and the relief is powerful. If I don't drink, I don't obsess about the amount of drinks in the bottle. The Machine doesn't get cranked up. I turned off my Machine. This week you get to feel for yourself what it's like to shut your Machine down for a while.

The Hangover Machine

For years if I woke up without a hangover—meaning refreshed, rested and not feeling as though a feral badger had given birth to its litter in my mouth—I was stunned. Most mornings I'd moan into my pillow and try to piece together the series of bad decisions that resulted in the familiar feeling that I'd been hit by a car while suffering from the flu.

Like most drunks, I had a Machine for hangovers too. If I had it together I would make sure I had at least eight ounces of water waiting for me by my bed. I would instantly slug it back and then stumble into the bathroom where I would take multiple Advil Liqui-gels. (The Liqui-gels work faster than the tablets.) After showering and getting dressed, I'd head to the kitchen to find some leftovers. Cereal wouldn't cut it.

If it was a workday, and five out of seven were, I would have two or three cans of Coke Classic before leaving for the office, and then several more while sitting at my desk. I counted the minutes until I could reasonably order lunch from the diner next door. Then it was greasy chicken fingers, more Coke, more Advil and I was finally, by noon or so, ready to tackle the day.

If I had a meeting in the morning that pre-empted me from hiding out in my office, I would sit there convincing myself that no one noticed how bad off I was.

If the hangover lingered throughout the day, I'd take a power nap before dinner and start all over again with a glass of chardonnay no later than 6 p.m.

Hangover management is no way to spend a life. Every day was the same. The problem was the same. The solution was the same. And the cause was the same. Day in, day out, I moved from drunk to sick to ok and back again. Maintaining all of my Machines became the focus of my existence to the exclusion of everything else.

Ten Things I Missed Because I Was Hungover

1. *A baby shower for one of my best friends*
2. *A once-in-a-lifetime trek to the top of a peak at Machu Picchu*
3. *A holiday tea with my sisters-in-law*
4. *The third day of a conference my company paid for me to attend*
5. *A bike ride on the beach during a vacation at Hilton Head*
6. *A shopping trip with my girlfriends during a weekend getaway that I planned*
7. *Several planned kayaking and hiking trips*
8. *A plane home*

9. *My first day of work at my first job out of college*
10. *Every Saturday morning from the ages of 28 to 33, and most Sundays*

Try a Different Kind of Suffering

One of my favorite books about overcoming addiction is Susan Shapiro's memoir *Lighting Up: How I Stopped Smoking, Drinking, and Everything Else I Loved in Life Except Sex.*

Shapiro is a writer and journalism teacher living in New York City who was reliant on her alcohol and cigarette addictions in order to write, work and function. When she started working with her therapist, Dr. W., she explained how she had tried virtually everything to quit her addictions and had always failed. A friend of hers asked her what Dr. W's philosophy for quitting is, and she answers:

"Suffering."

It's a poignant response. The reason many of us, myself included, started drinking too much in the first place is because we're afraid of suffering. The anxiety of walking into a party full of strangers can be instantly mollified by a quick cocktail. The stress of a day at the office where the boss was too demanding, the presentation didn't go well or the deal fell through can be significantly softened by a bottle of Bordeaux. The annoyance of dealing with kids who don't listen, don't eat and don't sleep can be blissfully forgotten if you can mix yourself a margarita after they're finally in bed.

Alcohol provides an instant feeling of relaxation that makes all manner of life's difficulties much less troubling. The problem is that when you rely on alcohol to smooth over the rough edges of your life, you're not only divorcing yourself from your true life experience, but you're opening yourself up to the dangers of addiction.

The Buddhists and Shapiro's Dr. W have it right: life is about suffering. There are lessons to be learned in finding ways within you to deal with the inevitable problems that come with being a resident of this planet. If you're relying on an outside element to deal with the pains of everyday life you're telling yourself that you aren't interested in having a real experience. And the more you use external sources to comfort you, the less you will be able handle things on your own. Masterful living requires us to face our difficulties head on, suffer through them, and to come out the other side with character, courage and self-reliance. If you reach for a bottle when things get tough, you're not engaging in life.

This week, I encourage you to try a hefty dose of suffering. By suffering I don't mean trying to get through the shakes or hallucinations on your own—please see a doctor if these are the issues you are facing. But in those moments when the house is quiet and the day is done and you find yourself wanting a drink, suffer through the craving.

When you're at the party with your friends and everyone is getting loose, get yourself another glass of water or fruit juice and experience what it's like to be around your friends with a clear and unaltered mind. Take some deep breaths. Collect yourself. Think deeply about what you're feeling, and listen to your internal arguments. Acknowledge them and let them go.

Your Mind is Not to be Trusted

Beware: you should know that the alcohol-loving mind is a trickster. When I'm suffering through a craving, these are the things my mind tells me:

You've been so good. You deserve a drink.

It's not the end of the world if you stay home alone tonight and enjoy a bottle of wine. Who's going to know?

There's nothing else to do so you should start drinking.

Everyone else here is drinking. You'll look weird if you don't.

Drinking is a part of your lifestyle. You have to learn to drink responsibly sometime. Think of this as practice.

What's the big deal if you have a few drinks? You're not driving.

No one will notice if you get a little drunk.

It's early. If you start drinking now, you'll feel fine tomorrow.

Are you really never going to drink your favorite (chardonnay, gin and tonic, microbrew) again? That's not living. You're cutting yourself off from a life experience.

But you want it!

These are some pretty persuasive arguments from my perspective. But for the most part I'm able to listen, say the argument out loud and send it packing. Plus, I have created a useful list of things to do to distract me from drinking when I need it, and I have provided it for you at the end of this book.

You're Probably Addicted to Sugar

Did you ingest lots of sugar as a kid? Do you eat lots of sugary foods now, in addition to the amount you're drinking? You're probably a raging sugar-holic. It's important to recognize this if you decide to quit drinking permanently.

The body metabolizes alcohol and sugar in nearly the same manner, and alcohol addiction is the result of the same biochemical routine as the sugar addiction. They both manipulate your brain's ability to create a feel-good chemical called dopamine. The more you use sugar, the more your brain relies on it to make you motivated, happy, sexually excited, etc. When I first quit drinking I substituted with ice cream, chocolate, candy and pretty much any other sugary substance I could get my hands on. It was the only thing that made me feel normal.

You're going to have to be careful during your seven days not to overload on sweets. Not only is this bad for your waistline, but it can be as hard on your internal organs— your liver, for one—as alcohol.

Sweets can be defined as the obvious things like candy, baked goods, etc. But you should also be aware that bread, pasta, cereal, fruits and fruit juices also break down into hefty amounts of sugar when you're digesting.

In other words, now is the time to start introducing lots of leafy greens and whole grains into your diet. Plus, pack on the proteins and healthy fats. And eat as many "whole foods" as you can muster. (A whole food is defined as a food that's as close as possible to its original form, i.e., a raw carrot or an egg.)

Avoid processed foods. You need to step away from the Lean Cuisines, the Eggo waffles and the mid-day Snickers bars. Not only are these processed foods filled with sugar and sodium, but they are also jam-packed with chemicals (for fake flavoring), genetically modified ingredients (no one knows how these things will affect us long-term) and something called "cellulose" which is a highly-processed form of wood shavings used to bulk up the density of processed foods without adding calories.

While you're not drinking during your seven days, use the extra time to read the labels on the food items in your pantry or grocery cart. You may be shocked to find that you're not only drinking too much alcohol, but that you're also ingesting a whole host of other noxious chemicals that are degrading your health.

Changing your diet, like taking a break from drinking, can be challenging. I'm not promising that you won't be grumpy at first, and I'm not asking you to take on a complete overhaul of your diet this week. Pay more attention to what you're putting in your gullet. In the long run, if you're able to control your drinking and improve your diet, you're on a winning path.

I personally transitioned from voracious carnivore (meat at every meal) to locavore (someone who eats foods primarily derived from local sources) to vegetarian and now vegan over the course of about three years. It didn't happen overnight—like my drinking didn't stop overnight. It's been a fascinating, creative journey that has resulted in a weight that hovers around 110 lbs. (I'm 5' 4"), crazy-ridiculous amounts of energy (I exercise every day and regularly hike 10 miles or more) and a calmer outlook. This is anecdotal, of course, but there's plenty of science to back up the fact that a healthy diet leads to a healthy body and mind.

For additional reading on the alcohol/sugar connection along with great information on recommended foods, you should read *How to Quit Drinking Without AA* by Jerry Dorsman. This is a very informative and useful book that outlines several self-governed strategies for eliminating alcohol and sugar simultaneously.

I also rely heavily on *How to Cook Everything Vegetarian* by Mark Bittman. It's the best cookbook I've found for incorporating more whole foods into my diet.

How Habits Are Formed

Everyone who drives the same route to or from work or school over an extended period of time has had the experience of not remembering how they got from point A to point B. The drive becomes a trance. Like a waking dream, we zone out and do the whole thing without event thinking about it. That's because the drive has become a habit, and it is so deeply ingrained in your brain's wiring that you can actually do the drive without checking in to make decisions along the way.

That's how I was with drinking. There were days when I swore I wasn't going to have a drink, and then—whoops— before I even was consciously aware of what was happening, I had uncorked a bottle and poured myself a glass. And of course, being a bit of a tippler, once the wine had been poured what was the point of wasting it? There I was, drunk again before I even knew what hit me.

The mechanism in our brains that gets us home from work during an out-of-body experience is the same one that hardwires our habits. Our brains are full of senders and receivers called "synapses," which are highways that deliver messages sent by neurons. When you send the same message over and over again via your thoughts, these synapses create reinforced pathways in the brain that form an infrastructure for habitual thought patterns and behaviors.

When you do or think the same thing over and over again, your brain actually gets rewired to accommodate the new behavior or thought. The more you do the behavior or thought, the harder the wiring gets and the more it starts to influence your decisions, moods and personality.

These "neural pathways" are formed when we learn to walk, talk, read and ride a bike. Neural pathways are formed when we repeatedly tell ourselves we're beautiful, when we tell ourselves we're ugly, when we tell ourselves we're dumb, unworthy or smarter than everyone. Neural pathways form when we have a cup of coffee every single morning, take a walk every single afternoon or when we have a drink every single night.

This is good news. What I love about neural pathways is that, not only can they be formed by repetition, thereby being very useful for learning new things like ice skating, but they can also be *unformed* by no longer engaging in a bad habit (like drinking) and replacing it with a newer, healthier habit (like walking).

You can re-wire your negative body image by telling yourself you're gorgeous just the way you are. You can re-wire your motivation to exercise by exercising more. You can give yourself a positive mental outlook by repeating positive messages over and over again—even if you don't believe them yet.

This also means that you can change your drinking habits for the better by *changing them*. It's as easy as you want it to be. Just change your habit. Instead of reaching for a bourbon, make a pot of tea. Instead of mixing a cocktail, blend a smoothie. Keep repeating the new habit relentlessly and your brain will re-wire itself. It's a case of fake-it-'til-you-make-it and it *works*.

This ability to reroute neural pathways is one reason that Alcoholics Anonymous works so well for certain problem drinkers, in my opinion. We'll talk about AA later in the book, but if you know anything at all about this group you know that they are known for repeating the same statements over and over again. It is my belief that repetition is effective for breaking the habits of drinking because AA members are re-wiring their neural pathways to help them overcome their habit.

Habit vs. Addiction

Alcohol habits are behavioral; alcohol addictions are physiological. They are both levels of severity on a very slippery slope.

My alcohol *habit* is what had me yearning for happy hour, my post-workout cocktail and the first drink of the party. It was a habit for me to have a glass in hand and to sip from it. The physical habit manifested the need to get the glass, fill it up and *make sure it stayed full* for as long as humanly possible. This is how I behaved around alcohol.

My alcohol *addiction* is what made it impossible for me to sleep without wine in my system. My addiction is what made my dark mood unbearable until my first drink of the day. My addiction is what gave me headaches, anxiety and stress when I wasn't drinking. My addiction also made it impossible for me to quit for a long time. It wasn't just my hand that wanted a glass, my body eventually needed the alcohol in order to regulate itself.

When we think of our drinking habits we rarely think of ourselves as addicted. There's a stigma attached to the word "addiction" or "addict" when it comes to boozing although people readily will admit they are "addicted" to coffee, chocolate or shopping.

I personally have no problem with admitting that I am addicted. I am addicted to alcohol, and it only took about three years of habitual drinking for my addiction to blow up out of control.

If you drink regularly your body is addicted to alcohol on some level. It's important to recognize this, especially if, at the end of the seven days, you decide to continue drinking. I encourage you to be mindful of the addiction trap with alcohol. No one, except the most meager drinkers or teetotalers, avoids it. Alcohol is addictive and the addiction is progressive, so you need to be careful.

Do you know anyone who has been a high-functioning heavy drinker for most of his or her life? This person is usually successful as far as being able to hold down a job, have friends, own a home and participate in some hobbies. For the most part, he's doing okay. But he drinks. A lot. I've seen more than a few of these types of drinkers transition from their 40s to their 50s and into their 60s. The 40s are usually all disposable income and fun and games, punctuated by a few killer hangovers. The 50s see their bodies get flabby, their buzzes get sloppy and their relationships get strained. Their finances start to suffer. In their 60s, they have heart attacks, strokes, shingles, cholesterol problems and a host of other health issues usually caused or exacerbated by drinking. None of these things convinces them to quit. They've never addressed drinking as a problem or even considered how alcohol may be affecting them. They only know now that they have to hide bottles from their wives, drink extras in the bedroom when their friends are over and otherwise be sneaky to get the drinks they think they "deserve." They can't get through a night at the movies, a sporting event or a dinner with friends without copious drinks. They cruise into their 70s, buzzed and sick. They don't usually live much longer.

I've seen this series of events unfold with friends and family, and the story is always the same. These people all start out in their teens or 20s with a little party habit that turns into a minor addiction. Decades later they're in full-blown addict mode and it's nearly too late to fix it. It snuck up on them so slowly and insidiously that even the people closest to them might not recognize that there is a problem. Nobody sees them as being an addict who needs help—they're elderly and people give them a pass or make lighthearted jokes about their "Drunkle Bill."

It's a shame because many of these folks could have enjoyed longer, more vigorous lives if they had realized they were on a slow train to disease. The progress is plodding, but the consequences can be terrible.

My Experiences with Blackouts

I recently tuned in to an episode of Celebrity Rehab (a show where famous people enter a drug and alcohol treatment facility and their therapy is made into a reality program) where one of the patients was asked if she had ever "blacked out" while drinking. She didn't know what this meant, so the doctor explained that blackouts are what happen when you drink until you can't remember what you've done. The patient was alarmed when she realized that this doesn't happen to everyone. She had blackouts every time she drank and thought this was normal.

Blackouts are not normal. If you're drinking so much that you can't remember several hours of the evening, how you got home (or wherever you ended up), who you're with or anything else, you need to take a good, hard look at your drinking.

Blackouts became part of my normal drinking process. On a "regular" evening entertaining friends at home, it wasn't unusual for me to lose whole conversations. On more exciting evenings out, I engaged in all kinds of behaviors that were a shock to me when they were brought up over a hangover breakfast. I always laughed my escapades off, chalking them up to collateral damage, but deep down I knew something was terribly wrong.

I have a recurring dream where I wake up in a hotel room next to someone I've presumably had sex with a few hours before. I do not know him, but I know the hotel because I've stayed there on business travel several times before. I remember meeting him in the hotel bar, but I don't remember coming to the room or anything that happened afterward. I gather my things to sneak back to my room before he wakes up. After fumbling through the halls, desperately trying to remember my room number and groping through my pockets to find my key card, I locate my room, let myself in, and fall asleep. As I drift off, I am overcome with shame.

I have this dream several times a year, and it's so vivid when I'm in it that I'm sure it's actually happening. The scary part is, I think it may have actually happened, and I have absolutely no recollection in my waking life that this occurred. Am I remembering part of a blackout? Or is it my subconscious trying to remind me that drinking is a dangerous game for me? I have no idea, and I probably never will.

Questions to Consider:

What part of The Machine is at work in your own drinking?

Are you managing your Machine or is it managing you? Is it something you want to keep in your life?

What suffering are you avoiding when you drink? Is the thought of not drinking painful for you? Which is worse?

Have you tried to quit and failed? What memories or feelings made you start drinking again?

Do you experience blackouts?

Have you experienced cravings? What worked to help eliminate them?

What sugary foods do you eat on a daily basis? What could you replace with a healthier choice?

Do you have a habit that can be changed or are you flirting with addiction?

What myths about your own drinking were you able to let go of today?

☙

Day Five:

Your Drinking Habits Aren't Your Fault (But They Are Your Responsibility)

When you gamble with drinking, the deck is stacked against you. From the societal acceptance of heavy drinking, to the fact that alcohol itself is a terribly addictive substance, that you drink excessively isn't surprising in the least. That some people never drink at all never ceases to astound me. I mean, *how do you avoid it?* Anytime an open bottle was in the vicinity I found myself skipping toward it.

It's Day Five, and you're getting a better sense of what your life might be like if you don't drink as much. You probably have more energy and some of your anxieties are starting to subside. Now that you've got a clear head, it's a good time to take a look at our culture of drinking.

What the Alcohol Industry Doesn't Want You to Know

I worked in the alcohol industry for more than a decade, so I'm fairly well educated in the persuasions, justifications and outright deceit alcohol marketers engage in. They spend billions of dollars to convince us all that alcohol is sexy, upscale, fun, and healthy in moderation. The most ludicrous assertion I've seen is that the farms where alcohol-producing crops are grown (particularly vineyards) are good for the environment.

Let's take each one of these ideas and break them down to understand what's really going on.

Alcohol is Sexy

I love alcohol ads because they are always filled with impossibly gorgeous creatures doing impossibly sexy things. Like dancing to a record player in Paris. Or playing poker in Armani suits. Or, for that matter, spiking beach volleyballs while wearing bikinis. Drinking is so sexy!

Or is it? I'll spare you the medical facts about how long term alcohol use can result in male impotence and loss of female sex drive. I'll even spare you the photos of what people look like when they've been drunk for most of their lives—the bruising, the bad skin, the broken capillaries, the nasty teeth. Instead I'll point out a few anecdotal things to get you thinking about alcohol and sex a little differently.

If you weren't drunk would you:

> Take your clothes off in public?

> Dance seductively with a guy or girl you just met?

> Go to bed with a stranger?

> Go to bed with a co-worker?

> Go to bed with a friend you're not attracted to, but you're both drunk so what the heck?

> Cheat on your partner?

> Have sex with a new partner way too early in the relationship?

> Pass out before sex can even occur?

Behave like you were so sexy that no one could resist you?

Throw yourself at people who clearly aren't interested?

Call a friend/acquaintance/ex at odd hours to proposition them for sex?

Is any of this sexy behavior to you? Reading this while you're (presumably) sober, does any of this seem erotic?

If you've never engaged in any of this behavior while on a bender, then bravo! I wish I could say the same. Every single sexual mistake, misstep, embarrassment or disaster I've ever experienced happened while I was drinking. There's nothing sexy about any of it. Especially when you wake up the morning after a sexcapade and you can't find your purse, or your keys, or your car, or your dignity. That's sexy, alright.

Drinking is an Upscale, Adult Activity and You've Earned It.

You work hard for your money. You deserve to indulge in a delicious adult beverage at the end of a long day, long week or during a grueling business lunch.

It's hard to argue with this spin since it is the prevailing marketing position of almost every alcoholic beverage available today. You can't turn on the television without seeing celebrities or characters that are richer than you over-indulging in their drink of choice. Snooki, Don Draper, The Real Housewives of Kerplunkistan… these people make drinking seem aspirational. Or at the very, very least not that big of a deal. Rappers sell their own private label booze. So do rock stars and actors.

Something I've noticed lately is that in many of the movies I'm watching, the hero or heroine has some kind of major breakthrough during a night of heavy boozing. Natalie Portman couldn't make the necessary transition into the Black Swan until she got drunk with the more passionate, live-on-the edge character played by Mila Kunis. (All the most fun-loving, free spirited and happy characters in movies tend to drink or do drugs...) In *Cedar Rapids*, Ed Helms plays a naïve insurance salesman who lives a sheltered, delusional existence until he gets hammered at a conference and "discovers" his "real self." William Powell and Myrna Loy in *The Thin Man* movies managed to elevate recreational drinking to an oh-so-witty art form. And Homer Simpson famously declared "*Ahh, beer. The cause of, and the solution to, all of my problems*." And this is a pathetically partial list...

It looks like everyone who is anyone drinks recreationally, and many of them have revelatory experiences while blitzed out of their minds. If these people get to do it, we should get to, too. If they're wearing the latest fashions, we should, too. If they travel to Ibiza twice a year, we should, too. We deserve it.

It's time for a shift in that "we deserve it" mentality. I would like to assert that we deserve better.

Why is it that when we have completed a tough assignment or have otherwise finished something good in our lives, we immediately think to "reward" ourselves with something that we know is unhealthy? If we're good we congratulate ourselves with that ice cream sundae even though we know it's fattening. We buy those boots, that watch, the new dress, even though our credit cards are maxed out. Or, we pour ourselves a massive drink, raise the glass and take a swig, even though we know that tomorrow we're going to pay the price with a hangover, the anxiety of all the embarrassing things we said or did or the worry that we wasted yet another night on the couch getting wasted.

I propose that during these seven days, you reward yourself with things that are actually rewarding. If you have a rough day, treat yourself to a massage. Great day? Go for a hike in a beautiful park and tuck yourself into bed early. Completed a life goal? Sign up for that exercise boot camp you've always wanted to take—you can do it.

It sounds really hokey, I know. And as one of those people who always loved to reward myself with a night of boozing, I understand how you're probably sitting there thinking that this is completely ridiculous. You're an adult. Adults drink to celebrate. Adults don't go for walks and snuggle into bed early. That's what little kids do.

I would have thought that, too until I did it, and I realized that when I have a rough day or a great day I deserve so much more than a foggy haze, the stress of wondering whom I've offended and a hellacious morning headache. In AA they have a saying: "Less drama. More laundry." Get on board with that this week. Be boring. What have you got to lose? It's just seven days… And you do deserve more.

Alcohol is Fun

Alcohol IS fun! Until it isn't anymore. But let's give alcohol some props for what it did for us in the early days of our drinking. I personally have alcohol to thank for the following positives:

> Getting me over my fear of social situations

> In the case of wine, opening my palate to a variety of different flavor combinations when paired with food

Also in the case of wine, gainful employment for over ten years

A look into agricultural processes, sustainability and environmentalism that I may not have otherwise had

The enjoyment of conversation with friends who were also drinking. When things are a little lubricated the conversations can be hilarious

The courage to sing karaoke pretty much anywhere

I also have alcohol to thank for the following negatives:

Extremely embarrassing behaviors, like singing karaoke pretty much anywhere

Regret for spreading gossip and/or lies I probably would have kept to myself had I not been lit

Anxiety that I would get fired for drinking too much at company functions

Hundreds of wasted weekend days spent sleeping off hangovers

The realization that the reason some people get DUIs at 8 a.m. is because they're still drunk from the night before. (I did not get a DUI, but I did drive drunk to work—as a result of the previous evening's "fun"—on more than one occasion)

Picking fights over silly things in my relationships, and then not understanding or remembering why my partner was upset

Calling in sick to work, missing appointments and having trouble staying awake during the workday

Weight gain and high cholesterol from a diet made up of "hangover foods" like burritos, burgers, fries and other greasy fast food

For me, alcohol was fun in the beginning. I got over my control issues and made friends. Drinking friends! I learned about a fascinating industry that I would eventually work in and have some real success. And I threw some unbelievable parties.

But it stopped being fun when the effervescent giddiness made way for a dark and sloppy reality. The loopy singing and dancing, the dopey clumsiness—all of that was pretty cute when I was 26. When I realized that I had trouble with my short-term memory, that I had no energy during the day and that the fights I started with my spouse no longer led to zesty makeup sex (they eventually led to divorce), I had to admit I was no longer having fun.

I suspect that since you ordered this book, you've turned a corner where alcohol isn't delivering on the fun promises it made to you in the early days. It can be exhausting! So stick with the program. With a sober mind you should be able to face the reality of whether or not drinking is still fun for you, and then you can make an informed decision about how you want to proceed.

Alcohol in Moderation is Healthy

Despite hundreds of alcohol industry-funded studies that claim that moderate drinking is good for you, it's simply not true. It's just not as bad for you as outright alcohol abuse.

Just because people who drink no more than "one 12-ounce bottle of beer or wine cooler, one five-ounce glass of wine, or 1.5 ounces of 80-proof distilled spirits"* per day are less likely to have problems—or to experience "few" problems—doesn't erase the fact that alcohol is a known toxin that damages your body. Plus, the reality is that no one just drinks one beer, one wine cooler, etc. If you can stop at one, you probably didn't start to begin with. Remember: alcohol is extremely addictive. It also dehydrates you so you naturally drink more, and so on and so forth. I have yet to meet anyone who drinks who fits the criteria of "moderate drinker" as described by the National Institute on Alcohol Abuse.

In 1991, *60 Minutes* did a segment on what they called "The French Paradox." The segment revealed that despite the unusually high amount of fats in the French diet—and the smoking—French people had a much lower rate of heart disease than Americans. One of the conclusions drawn from this investigation was that it must be the red wine the French consume.

Red wine contains a compound known as "resveratrol" and the wine industry in particular extols this specific compound as the silver bullet for heart disease. What they don't mention is that regular grape juice has as much or more resveratrol as red wine without the liver-killing alcohol. Dark chocolate and peanuts have about half the amount of resveratrol.

What the alcohol industry also would not like you to figure out is that, yes, the French diet is filled with fat, but it's usually straight butter fat primarily derived from organic dairies, not the hormone-laden butter, trans fats and corn oil fat of which Americans are so fond. Or they're getting their fat from cheese. Plus, the French eat very little processed food, and most of their food is grown within 100 miles of where they live. (Basically, the entire agriculture industry there was created to support the population of Paris.)

The French eat smaller portions of everything and eat their biggest meal in the middle of the day, not right before bed. They only work 35 hours a week, have five weeks government-mandated vacation, and socialized medicine that allows them access to preventative treatments. I haven't taken more than five days off per year in 18 years of full-time employment—how about you? (I currently have 15 weeks of unused vacation time.) Plus, I went to get a simple blood test a few months ago and was charged $750 for the privilege. (I have health insurance!) We do not encourage prevention in the US.

And Parisians walk. Everywhere.

There are several differences to the French lifestyle that can be called out as being the reasons for their lower heart disease rate. But the alcohol industry wants you to believe you need booze for heart health. They're lying. If you're really concerned about your heart, put down the drink and go for a walk.

Other health problems you might face from using alcohol:

Liver damage

Kidney failure

Cancer

Impotence

Memory loss

Heart disease

Stroke

High blood pressure

Suicide

Domestic violence

Traffic accidents

Sleep interruption

Depression

Anxiety

…And that's just a few.

One More Thing…

To put a finer point on the "Alcohol in Moderation is Healthy" lie, we must address the comprehensive study released in 2017 by the American Institute for Cancer Research and the World Cancer Research Fund. Not only did this study confirm a linear dose response in regards to amount of alcohol consumption and cancer risk (meaning your risk goes up as your drinking increases), but it was the first study to find a definitive link between any amount of alcohol consumption and breast cancer in women. Just one

10 oz. glass per day can increase the breast cancer risk by five percent in pre-menopausal women and nine percent in post-menopausal women.

In fact, as a collateral point, the news around this study brought to light that alcoholic beverages are classified as a Class One Carcinogen. This means that there is a proven link between drinking and cancer.

Do you know what other things are classified as Class One Carcinogens? Cigarettes, arsenic, plutonium and asbestos. Yikes.

And what drives me crazy about the media's narrative about alcohol's Class One rating, is that they continually interview doctors and experts who emphasize in sympathetic quotes that "no one is telling you that you shouldn't drink at all. Just be moderate." Okay. I guess I can just be moderate with smoking, arsenic consumption, handling plutonium and breathing asbestos, as well? It's nuts. But this is also an indicator of how sick we are as a culture as far as our dependence on alcohol is concerned. We have proof that alcohol is as likely to cause cancer as *plutonium*, but the experts are telling us it's cool to keep drinking sometimes. Sure, guys (she says, as she deeply inhales some asbestos...).

No amount of alcohol is "healthy." Drinking less does less damage, but that's like saying jabbing yourself with scissors does less damage than slicing yourself with a sushi knife. Why would you want to do either?

From the National Institute on Alcohol Abuse and Alcoholism

The Wine I Drink is Good for the Environment

This is by far my favorite fallacy and the one I know the most about, so excuse me if I go off here. Wine may not be your poison of choice, but it was mine, and I have a real insider's look at how the public relations wonks at these companies make us believe that drinking wine is grown up, responsible and environmentally sound.

I've personally worked many late nights to publicize the feel-good things wineries claim in regards to the environment. "Our vineyards provide habitat to several species," they claim. "We're [organic, sustainable, biodynamic], so our wines are low impact on the environment," they write. "Our bag-in-box packaging is recyclable..."

Many of the environmental blogs I read have weekly or monthly columns where they recommend "green" wines, and they're often repeating the BS talking points that all so-called sustainable, organic or biodynamic wineries tout.

Let me make this clear: there are no wineries that are good for the environment. Wineries tear up mountaintops for their vineyards and bore holes in hillsides for their wine caves. Wastewater ponds are filled with toxic gunk. The rip out heritage oak woodlands with impunity. They drain rivers to water their grapes and protect the buds from frost, leaving the local trout with no place to spawn. These protected fish bloody themselves by slamming their bodies against exposed rocks while trying to lay eggs in drained rivers.

In the wine region where I live wineries have taken over all of the farmland. Where we previously had orchards filled with several unique varieties of apples and pears, there are wine grapes. Where we used to have farms with rotating seasonal abundance that fed the local population, we now have nothing but wine grapes and grocery stores that ship in food from Mexico, South America, New Zealand and China. These wineries have created a monoculture in a region that was at one time one of the most fertile and diverse foodsheds in the world.

One of the wineries I worked for made a daily practice of violating the Federal Migratory Bird Act by trapping and drowning thousands of finches in their vineyards because they ate the grapes. This particular winery's website has several beautiful sections heralding its sustainable practices and environmental stewardship.

The only no impact winery is the winery that never got built. Don't fool yourself into thinking that you're imbibing a product that was made by people who care about the Earth. They talk a big game, but the vast majority of wine companies (which are often part of huge, publicly traded corporations) tout their environmental sensitivity when really they're just interested in their own profits. I know. I've seen it first hand.

Lies—Oops, I Mean *Reasons*—We Tell Ourselves About Why We Drink

We all have reasons we think we "need" or "want" to drink. I'm here to tell you that they are all lies. No reason for drinking is actually *helped* by drinking. The best-case scenario is that the drinking has a neutral effect on your outcome. The worst-case scenario is that the drinking actually makes your situation worse.

This is not a scientific list, only a compilation of the things I've seen when dealing with people who drink. You may see yourself reflected in the sentiments below. Or, you may not see your favorite on here at all. As part of your exercise, I encourage you to think about the lies that may be at work in your life in regards to why you drink.

I need to unwind from my stressful job. You're not going to get any argument from me that work is stressful. In fact, with the current economic situation work seems to be getting even worse. Not only are our benefits being cut, our hours are getting longer and the demands on our abilities increasing—and we're also supposed to be grateful for our jobs. Don't even get me started on dirtbag healthcare plans, unfair scheduling and draconian family leave policies. Plus, with our long commutes, our eating on-the-go and endless hours sitting or standing, work is causing our health to suffer. I don't think anyone would disagree that work can drive us to drink.

Alcohol does give you a quick and simple way to feel mellow and relaxed after a long day at work. But alcohol also makes you feel fatigued rather than energized. Alcohol may help you drift off to sleep, but it messes with your ability to fall into a deep and restful slumber—which makes it even harder for you to wake up in the morning. It also contributes to the desire for caffeinated, sugary beverages that give a quick spike of energy, but also lead to severe crashes.

Better stressbusters include taking a brisk half-hour walk or taking a quick nap. There are also herbal teas that can help you take the stress level down in a way that provides a sense of refreshment rather than dullness. You may not like the sound of these choices at first because they require a bit of effort on your part. But the fact that other proven stress-relief methods exist proves that your "need" for alcohol to unwind is a lie you tell yourself to keep drinking.

I need a quick way to relax because I have kids. I know lots of women who use alcohol as a mommy's little helper. It's readily available without a prescription, it's socially acceptable (and often encouraged) and it gives a feeling of being an "adult" after a day spent with people who aren't really designed for grown-up interaction. The problem is when your glass after the kids go to bed turns into a glass before dinner, a glass before they come home and a water bottle full of wine at their soccer game. It's a slippery slope, and if you're home alone with the children all day it's easy to hide the amount that you are really drinking. Be careful here.

Having kids is stressful and isolating. But there are other ways to manage the difficulty that won't put you or your kids in harm's way. Making some time for exercise, taking a nap when the kids do, and engaging in quiet time activities with them can help. If you're struggling with being overscheduled take a look at your calendar to see the things that you could possibly eliminate.

Also, if your playdates with other moms and kids are turning into excuses for the mommies to mix margaritas it might be time to take stock in how you want to be spending your time. Raising kids is tough and draining, but I can promise you that you don't want to look back on your kids' childhoods and wonder why all of the memories are clouded in a salt-rimmed haze.

When you have children it's important to keep your head clear. Your stress level is not going to decrease if something bad happens to one of your kids and you're too buzzed to handle it appropriately. That's not going to relax you one bit.

I like to party. Well, who doesn't? It's when your desire to gather together with friends becomes less about connecting and socializing and more about drinking and getting out of control that you may need to think about what your drinking is bringing to the party. It's good to cut loose and act a little crazy sometimes. Everyone needs to blow off steam with nights of big fun. But when your partying results in blackouts, ending up in seedy places, sleeping with people you just met or having screaming matches in the parking lot, you may have tipped from "party" to "insanity." Think about the last time you were able to go out for a night on the town without drinking. Has that ever happened?

What is it that you like about partying, really? Is it the dancing, the flirting, the silly jokes, the bonding with friends? Or is it what you find at the bottom of your glass? If it's the former, then you don't need to drink when you party, do you?

Everyone drinks. Maybe everyone around you drinks, but the fact remains that as of 2010, 43% of adults in the United States considered themselves teetotalers according to a Gallup Poll conducted in July of that year.

So not everyone drinks. A majority of US adults do, to be sure, but it's not true that everyone drinks. Forty-three percent of us never do.

Even though both of my parents never drank alcohol or even had any alcohol in the house, I still find it astonishing that there are people out there who never drink. I mean, they aren't even *interested* in drinking. But the numbers are there—almost half the country's adults don't drink. So that means that if "everyone" around you drinks chances are you're seeking out people with the same behaviors as you. Would you be comfortable hanging out with people who don't drink?

I wasn't. I would make mental notes about people who didn't drink and would make sure to avoid them. I always thought that non-drinkers weren't any fun. What I found out after being sober for a while was that the feeling was mutual.

I drink to network for job opportunities. I saw an episode of the TV show *Friends* where Rachel took up smoking because her boss was a smoker, and she handed out promotions to the underlings who would step out for z mid-morning drag with her.

If that seems insane to you, that's because it is.

It's true that we sometimes have to do things for our jobs that are counter to good sense. But there's no job that's worth destroying your health for. You don't need the drinks for networking, but you may need to participate in the after work gathering, the weekend golf outing or the corporate retreat. If these are events where lots of drinking happens it's a good bet that no one will notice if you are drinking or not. I seriously doubt anyone ever got promoted for being a drunk. So drinking for work is yet another lie.

I drink to escape the pain from a traumatic event, difficult childhood, bad marriage, etc. So many people drink to ease the pain of something terrible that has happened in their lives. If this is the case for you, please consider getting the help of a professional therapist to deal with these feelings. What happens when we drink to handle problems that are too big for us to manage on our own, is that the drinking becomes an even bigger issue—an issue that needs to be solved before you can even begin to address the real problem. Drinking to deal with pain over a prolonged period of time leads to alcoholism.

I only drink because my spouse or partner drinks. My ex-husband admitted to me that sometimes he drank "ahead" of me to keep me from drinking so much. He would pour himself extra so I couldn't have it. I initially responded to this with anger because I hated the idea that he was drinking *my* booze! But over time I realized that he was—in a very unhealthy way—attempting to look out for me. If this is the reason you're drinking, you need to take a good hard look at your relationship to determine if: 1) you're worried about the amount your partner is drinking, or 2) you're worried that both of you may have a drinking problem.

Some couples drink together because they are caught in a pattern of avoiding a real connection. If you met while drinking, fell in love while drinking, fight while drinking, make up while drinking, celebrate while drinking, etc., there's a distinct possibility that you're using alcohol to not only avoid real feelings, but to also create drama in a relationship that may otherwise seem stale.

Every one of my adult relationships started and ended with drinking. I found that I was able to forgive any manner of personality defects (his and mine) as long as he'd show up with a bottle of wine or two. Now that I'm sober and in a very loving relationship I can tell you that it is not always easy without the hazy blur of alcohol to gloss over all of the warts and pimples (his and mine). But I do know that the relationship we have created is based on real feelings, real moments and real, honest reactions to what's really happening. And best of all, I almost always remember our conversations.

If you feel pressured to drink to deal with your relationship, I invite you to spend your seven days observing how your relationship changes while at least one of you is sober. You may be surprised at what you find out.

I enjoy the taste. Having been steeped in the wine industry for a decade of my life, I have experienced first hand all the ways we talk ourselves in to loving the taste of alcohol. The wine industry has created an entire sub-industry of people who make their living breaking down the flavor profiles of wines and then assigning them awards for deliciousness.

The beer industry is coming around to this, too, with reviews, competitions, and the rise of "artisan" small-lot brewers. Mixmasters the world over have created thousands upon thousands of sugary concoctions to help drinkers get a dose of hard alcohol, which, when served on its own, is totally revolting.

The funny thing is most people, when blindfolded, can't even tell if a wine is red or white or if they're drinking vodka or gin or if their beer is a stout or an IPA. It's true! Try it yourself if you don't believe me—but only after your seven days is up.

Think about that. If you love the taste so much, if it's so delicious to you, why can't you tell what it is when you're blindfolded? Why doesn't it give you the same visceral reaction as, say, a cola? (People can tell a cola vs. a citrus-based soda when blindfolded, just maybe not whether it's Coke or Pepsi…)

If these bevvies didn't make us feel a certain way we probably wouldn't drink them at all. If booze didn't make us lose our inhibitions, become silly and help us hide from our real emotions, most of us wouldn't touch it. During my drinking days, I definitely got to the point every night where I could care less what the drink tasted like, I just wanted more. I never "loved" the taste, but the flavor of certain alcoholic beverages certainly summoned a particular feeling that I couldn't get with water, soda, coffee or tea. I was always willing to sacrifice flavor for the buzz. Think about whether or not that's the case for you. I mean, when was the last time you felt like you should cut back on the water?

Drinking is how I celebrate life. All of life's milestones seem to be punctuated by the need to drink. Weddings must be accompanied by a toast. Winning an award calls for a round of drinks. Getting a new job, buying a new house, having a baby—all of these things can lead to popped corks. We even warn newly graduated teenagers not to drink and drive and they aren't even of legal drinking age! It's assumed that because something great has happened we all need to celebrate with alcohol.

The problem with this line of thinking, especially with heavy drinkers, is that we become unable to enjoy any of life's smaller pleasures without the accompaniment of alcohol. Friday happy hours turn into Saturday morning Bloody Marys. Thursday night movie night requires several gin and tonics. Hanging out with friends means that you need to stop and pick up a six-pack.

I would like to propose that perhaps drinking is not how you celebrate life, it's how you manage to deal with all of the pressures that are inherent in modern living. The fact is that life is hard, reasons to celebrate can be few, and alcohol provides a quick, zippy emotional feeling that helps you to cut loose and feel like you don't have to worry so much anymore.

But this is not a celebration. Waking up with the sunrise and going for stroll along the river is a celebration. Playing with your kids on a lazy Sunday afternoon is a celebration. Preparing a meal, going for a run, learning a new skill— these things are the true celebrations of why we are here on this planet. I promise you one thing: on your deathbed you will never look back and wonder why you didn't drink more.

The Second Time I Tried to Quit

After my therapist took me to AA, and I worked so hard to remain sober for almost two years, I started drinking again. I had been in a relationship, mostly sober (there was one little three-day-weekend hiccup), for almost a year. We were happy, functioning and everything was going great. We moved in together, and slowly I began re-introducing wine into my life.

First it was little celebratory sips here and there. I'd toast my new job or our new place. Then it was a shared bottle on a Friday night while watching a movie. Then there were friends coming over for dinner and games—an excuse to really go all-out. What was great about this, in my opinion, was that my drinking pattern was nothing like before. I didn't drink every night; I wasn't waking up with hangovers every day. I was cool. I was a moderate drinker! For a while anyway.

Even though I seemed to be able to maintain respectability for the most part, I had a tendency to go off the rails at times when you'd least expect it. There was the business trip where I didn't drink at all (so proud!) until the last night and then ended up naked in the pool with about 20 other people. It took about three days to recover from that hangover.

There was the class reunion I went to with my boyfriend that I don't remember at all, except the part where he grabbed me and said "Time to go." And so on.

I had managed my daily drinking, but the binges were epic. So, I quit. Again. This time I had an exceedingly supportive partner. I'm not sure how long I stayed sober this go-round, but it wasn't very long...

Questions to Consider:

Have you ever really considered how addictive alcohol is? Were you aware of the dangers of continued drinking?

How have you been fooled by clever marketing campaigns?

Are there any movie characters or celebrities that inspired your drinking?

What positives has alcohol brought to your life? What negatives?

Do the health ramifications of years of drinking worry you? Or do you feel like the amount you drink is moderate enough?

If you drink wine for the health benefits, would you be willing to switch to something that doesn't also have the negative effects?

What are the lies you tell yourself about why you drink? It's easy to talk yourself into believing them. Have you tried talking yourself out of them?

Day Six:

Managing Your Myths

Everyone lies about their drinking. There are the "I've only had two," or the "I never get hungover" lies that most people participate in every once in a while, but this doesn't concern me. It's the larger myths, the ones that contribute to a dysfunctional denial of our drinking habits, that I'd like us to explore now.

It CAN Happen to You

In my early days of drinking I remember saying out loud that I would do everything I could to prevent becoming an alcoholic because I loved drinking so much. I was young and beautiful with money and a prestigious job in the wine business. I had the world at my feet. I lived a lifestyle that was built around the luxury of fine food and wine, and it never entered my mind that I might get so addicted to alcohol that I would have night sweats every time I went to bed without having a drink, or that I would rush home from work at five o'clock sharp because the idea of one more minute without a glass of wine was excruciating.

If you had told me that I would find myself sleeping on my dog's bed in the garage several nights a week because I was too drunk to make it from the car to my own cozy bed I would have laughed in your face. (Let's not even discuss the DAILY drinking and driving…) No one told me that my dependence on alcohol would direct every decision I made from where I ate dinner, to what after work activities I would agree to, and what friends I would spend time with— but if they had I would have ignored their observation. If you had suggested that I would be nearly 40 before I was able to manage my drinking—and that I would still be struggling—I would have called you a liar or worse.

But all of that did happen to me. And here's why.

Aside from the relaxing effects, the delicious flavors, the ubiquitous presence and social acceptance of drinking alcohol, **alcohol is a viciously addictive substance**.

It's not your fault that you are struggling with alcohol. It is not a character flaw or a moral failing. I'll even go so far as to go against prevailing wisdom: addiction to alcohol is not even a disease, although it's clear that some people do seem to have a different biological reaction to alcohol than others.

I'm going to say the thing that no one wants to admit, that the marketers cover up and that even the most sympathetic therapists have a hard time saying: **alcohol is an addictive substance**. It's as addictive, or more so, than cigarettes and illegal drugs. The problem is that nearly everyone is in denial about how dangerous the addictive qualities of alcohol are because it is a socially acceptable, moneymaking machine.

Denial is Destructive

In our culture, denial about the problems caused by alcohol is rampant. People do not want to accept that drinking is often the cause of relationship issues, health problems, mood disorders, personal failures and so many other things that aren't going well. Let's also be reminded of the media narrative that moderation is fine, despite a massive study that shows alcohol definitively, inarguably and absolutely causes cancer.

Your friends and family are possibly in denial because they can't admit that alcohol has them addicted, too. They want to keep drinking because of the same reason you do—it's a lot easier to let alcohol dull down the difficulties of life from work, family, health, relationships and whatever else is troubling them. Popping open a can or mixing a cocktail is a lot easier than facing their struggles or admitting their own role in the problems of their lives. It never ceases to amaze me how animated people can get when you even hint that drinking may not be such a good idea. You'll see this during your seven days if you choose to discuss it. Take note of the defensive reactions, the friends who no longer call or the family members who try to tease you. This will happen, and it's a result of their own denial of how strongly alcohol has them in its grasp.

Even some of the most skilled therapists have trouble identifying that alcohol is the problem and not something else, like a mental disorder or a character flaw. Why is this? Therapists make their money helping broken people heal. If the person isn't necessarily depressed, anxious or bipolar, just in the grips of a chemical, then the patient doesn't have much of a reason to go back after quitting, do they?

In my own family I've witnessed the deceit and damage caused by denying alcoholism as the basis of a problem. From the time I was born I was told that my paternal grandfather passed away at age 40 from a heart attack. When medical doctors asked me if there was a history of heart disease in my family I always told them that my grandfather had died at a very early age from a heart attack. For years, I was worried that perhaps there was something congenital that could be passed to me, but my questions to my family and my requests for testing fell on deaf ears. They'd get quiet, change the subject, look away…

I was in my mid-thirties before my mother let it slip that my paternal grandfather had died of a heart attack directly after my grandmother had left him because *his drinking was so out of control*.

My grandfather had died of a "heart attack" brought on by an overdose of alcohol. He drank so much his heart stopped beating.

In the meantime, both my brother and I grew up worried that we both have some heart flaw that's going to explode at any time. Plus, we both struggle with addiction.

While we were looking at the smoke in the mirror over here, there was a wolf hiding in the corner over there. Not one member of my family ever warned me of the threat of drinking, that I am probably genetically wired for alcoholism and that I need to be careful. They were so in denial that they were willing to offer me up to the wolves rather than face the truth.

People are in denial about drinking. I hope that during this sober week, you have the courage to face your drinking history head on.

Do you think it's possible that if you cleared the alcohol out of your life and spent time focusing on your issues rather than running away from them, that you may be able to find the contentment you seek? No matter what your life difficulties are, they are being compounded by alcohol, not helped. The admission that alcohol caused my problems, and the willingness to accept the idea that I am not inherently flawed, has made all the difference in the world to my own struggle. This realization clears the way for me to have real discussions about my depression and anxiety— discussions that don't revolve around lies or around my failures, shortcomings or mistakes.

The Myth of Intimacy through Imbibing

In Caroline Knapp's memoir, *Drinking: A Love Story*, she writes: "Alcoholics tend to drink alone even when they're drinking with other people." She recalls the story of a night of heavy drinking with some friends. She'd gone out with the sole purpose of "getting rip roaring drunk," and she more than accomplished her mission. She stayed up late into the night, and she woke up with a hellacious hangover. She realized, as she was lying there wishing she had an Advil, that she hadn't made eye contact with any of her friends during their conversation. She wondered, *"how you could spend an evening like that with an intimate group, and end up all alone, sitting in a circle around a café table with two other people and no one at the same time?"*

I used alcohol to form connections with people that I wouldn't have been able to build while sober. While I'm not shy, I am anxious and controlling, and I have trouble focusing. I have a lot of energy and my mind is fast and active. Trying to have a conversation with people while I'm sober can be very difficult for me. I'm thinking four steps ahead, I interrupt and I get overly enthusiastic about the points I want to make. I also get very tired because, frankly, I try way too hard to make people like me.

But when I drink my controlling nature melts away, my anxiety subsides and my mind slows down to where I can stay in the conversation without feeling like a racehorse ready to burst out of the gate. Once I start drinking I develop what one of my friends calls "Richard Marx Disease." What is that, you ask? "It's when you want to 'Hold on to the Night.'" I'll keep you up until you kick me out.

So many nights I've looked at the clock when it said 8 p.m. and then, in a flash, looked at it again and it was after midnight. Convinced that the conversation I was having was "special" and the person I was having it with "really wants to keep talking" and that the topic is "really changing my life," I would hold on to the night until dawn. I truly believed that the drunk conversations I had with people were intimate, interesting, revealing and revolutionary. I shudder to think what I would have seen if any of those conversations had been videotaped.

The tragedy for me is that, in nearly all of those cases, I couldn't remember what we even talked about the next day. More often than not I was really anxious or worried that I might have said something to offend someone, that I revealed someone else's secret (I did that a lot) or that I spent the whole time oversharing.

Despite those life changing late night conversations, true intimacy cannot be created through a liquid lens of alcohol. You can't see another person or be seen yourself when you've ladled a numbing chemical all over your brain.

When you choose to approach an interaction sober, you're choosing to bring your whole self to the table, not a chemically enhanced version of your persona. If you're anxious, be anxious. If you're bored, be bored (ask yourself why would you want to hang out with people who bore you to the point of needing a drink to deal with them?). If you're self-conscious, be self-conscious. Learn what it feels like to simply feel what you're feeling. Don't judge yourself. I assure you, no one has ever died of anxiety, boredom or self-consciousness. Plenty of people have died from drinking too much, though.

The Myth of Alcohol as Problem Solver

Before reading *Drinking: A Love Story* I had never made the connection that drinking was often the cause of my relationship worries, depression and stress.

My marriage was in trouble, so I needed a drink. My job was stressful so I needed a drink. My family is difficult, so I need to drink to be around them. I had gotten drunk and spilled a friend's secret—she was mad at me—so I needed a drink. I told myself I would quit drinking so much when things got better in my life. When things were better, I wouldn't need to drink.

It had never once occurred to me that the common thread throughout all of the things that brought me pain was drinking. Drinking did not smooth over these problems or make me more able to handle them. Drinking caused these problems.

Drinking made me unable to have a real conversation with my husband about our difficulties. Drinking made me feel sick and hungover so I couldn't attack my job with the gusto it deserved. Drinking made me over-exaggerate the issues with my family so that I could never just be with them. Drinking made me unable to discern what information was truly dear to someone and made me prone to spilling secrets in order to be the center of attention. While I was drinking none of these problems improved, so down the rabbit hole I continued to go.

At one point in her memoir, Knapp writes about being caught in a cycle of infidelity and dishonesty with two men while she was drinking, and it was the drinking that continued to lubricate her deceptive machine. She was involved with an older man she would meet in the middle of the day. They would drink martinis, and even though she had no real interest in him romantically the alcohol blurred her boundary lines so that she was unable to fend off his advances. In the evening, she would drink with the man with whom she was living and lie about her activities during the day. She was stuck, unable to make a change, and it was the alcohol that kept her there. Until she was able to approach her afternoon boyfriend sober, she wasn't able to break up with him. When she finally did, she felt nothing.

She writes: *"The amazing thing, of course, is that you do all this—all this drinking, all the keeping of secrets and withholding of information, all the self-medicating—without making the connections between the drink and the outcome."*

I look back on my relationships, including my marriage, and I am aghast at how many of them started while drinking and then continued on a trajectory of alcohol-fueled dramas, break ups, make ups... My marriage was so alcohol soaked that not only did our drinking cause all of our problems, but all of our happiest times were while drinking, too.

When I quit, I had already left him. We were trying to work things out, to get back together, but it became obvious that not only could the marriage no longer handle my drinking, but we also didn't have the connection we needed to support getting sober. I did not know how to relate to my husband without a glass of wine in my hand. When the river of booze finally dried up, there was nothing left but a rocky canyon that I no longer had the energy to traverse.

During your seven days of sobriety, I invite you to reflect on the relationships in your life that involve alcohol. How many dramas have been fired up when you're drinking, or worse, how many offenses have you overlooked because either A) they were drinking and couldn't help it B) YOU were drinking and couldn't help it C) both of you were drinking and couldn't help it?

Can you envision a life filled with relationships where you don't have to apologize, or wait for an apology, because you both were drinking? Can you envision a relationship that's built upon true mutual interest, trust and activities that bring you health, presence and awareness?

The Myth That You Cannot Change

One of the hurdles I faced when I first decided to stop imbibing was my inability to imagine myself behaving any other way. I had been a drinker for more than half my life. My drinking parties and escapades were (in my mind, anyway) legendary. My persona was so tied up in my ability to pound several gallons of alcohol at any occasion that letting it go was inconceivable to me.

It took an enormous amount of reflection to realize that this was all in my head. And not only was my persona something that I had concocted to make me feel less stressed in social situations, it had also become the crutch I used to keep myself from quitting for as long as possible. If other people expected me to drink, then who was I to disappoint them?

It was an excuse. The myth that I couldn't change my behavior was one of the biggest lies with which I wrestled. Once I saw it for what it was, my decision to stay sober got much easier.

Human beings are capable of making all kinds of sweeping changes. They can lose enormous amounts of weight, quit smoking, create healthy thought patterns… They can even quit drinking or using drugs. People can often accomplish this on their own. More often, they need to ask for help. If you believe you can't change, that's the biggest myth you've got working in your life—and I'm here to tell you it's not true.

The Myth That You Need Alcohol to Have Fun

I went to the roller derby one Saturday night and spent two glorious hours watching grown men and women (it was co-ed, inexplicably) zoom around a track wearing ridiculous outfits and trying to knock each other over. The crowd was filled with people like me who were attending with a firm grasp of the irony of the escapade. The crowd was also filled with people who had more fingers than teeth and would think that irony was the name of a joint disorder. The entertainment value of this experience ranked about 13 on a scale of 1 to 10.

I am an amateur figure skater, so I couldn't wait to tell my skating friends about this adventure. Being interested in skating I thought that they, in particular, would enjoy hearing all about roller derby. I described the sights, the costumes and the over-the-top drama and I invited my friends to join me for a crazy night out next time there was a match. The first response was:

"Can we drink? Do they sell alcohol at the rink? I guess I could smuggle in my own, but if they had it there that would be awesome. Drink and watch roller derby!"

I wasn't surprised, actually, although I was a bit disappointed. Roller derby is a raucous, loud, exuberant experience that needs no enhancement for it to be completely awesome. I didn't drink a drop and I'm still reeling from the excitement. Why does my friend feel like she needs to drink—even at the roller derby—to have fun?

I used to think this way, too, and it's not only because I have a physical addiction to alcohol, but I have an emotional addiction, too.

My anxiety and depression were so severe for so long that the first real relief I ever felt was when I started drinking regularly. I was crippled with fear of social situations, so I would drink to play well with others. It worked like a charm, and I quickly went from being an uptight killjoy to being the life of the party. The problem is that I didn't ever learn how to have fun sober as an adult so when the drinks dried up so did the good time.

I think many drinkers use this same pattern. I know that if I am anxious in social situations that other people must be, too, and they have used alcohol to help them deal with their fears. It has worked so effectively that they equate fun with drinking, and they might now sneak wine into movies (done it), take wine on hikes (done it), drink while boating (check) or drink at the roller derby (nope!) because they simply can't imagine loosening up enough to have fun on their own, without a drink.

Now that I'm sober I find that when people insist on drinking at events that are already designed for enjoyment, I'm a bit disturbed. Not judgmental or disappointed, really, but sad that they feel that they have to put a chemical in their body in order to have a good time.

I also think that many of us drink to enhance our experiences because we're trying to recapture a feeling of excitement about life that we haven't felt since we were children.

Remember when you were really small and you could experience unbridled joy at stomping on a mud puddle or spinning around until you fell over? Remember when everything was new, and that getting a new toy or watching your favorite movie over and over and over again could make you giddy? We lose that as we get older, that feeling of unfettered excitement, and I think we drink because drinking can manufacture that same enthusiasm.

I definitely felt that way. I always thought that drinking would catapult whatever experience I was having into something transcendent and blissful. It never did, but I kept trying, over and over and over again until the whole thing turned bonkers.

When I'm not drinking I have the awareness to take in my entire experience. When I'm in nature I feel truly present. When I'm at a show, I can focus on the lines, the songs and the performance. When I'm at dinner I take in every flavor rather than washing it over with alcohol, and I remember it the next day. I have a different kind of fun now, although I go to bed a bit earlier and I leave parties the minute I get bored. I have real conversations with people. I spend my time learning and achieving new things, which isn't always easy and sometimes it's embarrassing. And even though many people wouldn't describe my life as "free-wheeling fun" it's hard to deny that my life is now filled with contentment and satisfaction. And that's enough fun for me.

Third Time's the Charm: Quitting for Good

Even though I had experienced some disastrous binges and quit drinking twice, I picked up the bottle again. My life was very different by this time, so my pattern had changed completely. I think this is why, this time, it took several more months for me to realize that I was drinking alcoholically again.

My boyfriend and I had moved to a new town. I had a job where I worked from home with no business travel, hence no more crazy alcohol-fueled, on-the-road escapades. I had completely stopped drinking at social gatherings and had no problem getting through them with a glass of water in hand.

But I was drinking a lot at home. I may not have had wine at the party, but I'd swing by the corner market on the way home and pick up one or two bottles if it was still early. I no longer drank in front of family when they visited, but the minute they went to bed I popped a cork. I would go for hikes early on Saturdays, but I would have completed my first bottle of wine by 4 pm, and would buy more.

My drinking became an at-home-only thing (with the occasional glass when we went out to dinner), and it was getting increasingly destructive. The weekends-only policy eventually became Thursday through Sunday. Then I added in Wednesdays if it was a particularly stressful day. Tuesdays got added in as a joke. And when I rolled back to Monday because, well, what's one more day?

I would go for weeks like this, take a seven-day break, and start up again. On and on, round and round until I was blue, depressed and snappy all the time. I was sick of feeling sick and, frankly I was turning forty and I didn't want to spend the next half of my life trying to manage this shit anymore. I wanted it over.

What tipped me over to what I believe is now a much more comprehensive recovery is my work with a qualified hypnotherapist, my online support community, my belief in the tenets of AA, daily exercise, a healthy diet, continual study and research around addiction—and a belief that this is possible for me.

I finally discovered that my life works better without alcohol.

Questions to Consider:

Do you believe that you are addicted to alcohol?

What drinking myths have you believed until now?

How did believing these myths help you perpetuate your drinking?

Are there other lies you tell yourself to keep drinking?

What friendships have you formed while drinking? If you didn't drink would you still want those relationships?

What difficulties do you have that you think might be directly related to your drinking?

What relationships in your life would be improved if you drank less? Why?

Do you feel like you have to drink to have fun?

Day Seven:

What's Next?

It's your last day of sobriety—or is it? Today is your opportunity to take inventory of what you've learned this week to decide if you need another seven days, seven weeks, seven months or seven years.

I hope that you spent this week trying a few new things, reflecting on why you wanted to take a break from the bottle to begin with and enjoying a refreshed and renewed attitude. It took me several years of seven-day breaks to finally embrace full-time sobriety. But with this simple plan, a good dose of therapy and some very beneficial AA meetings, the switch finally flipped for me and I have remained quite happily sober.

I only have good things to say about that. If you decide to continue with your sobriety, I commend you and offer you this chapter filled with next steps to help make your journey as worry free as possible. If you're going to continue drinking alcohol, I invite you back to these pages any time you need them to help you through another seven days.

Why I Love AA

Any person thinking about cutting back on their drinking should go to an AA meeting, or two, or two hundred. My first AA meeting was a watershed moment in my understanding of alcohol abuse, not only because I felt warmly accepted by a room full of people who instantly understood my struggle, but because I knew or worked with about a third of the people in that room.

My first AA meeting was unique in that regard. In retrospect I probably should have realized that being in a small wine community meant that I would run into at least one or two other people I knew. But I was really naïve to the extent of the drinking problems that were running rampant through my industry. I felt both saddened and relieved by this realization. I was sad that this group of intelligent, interesting, lovable people were having such a difficult time, and I was relieved that I wasn't alone.

I had the element of surprise when I first walked in, and the immediate understanding that I was not the first, last, best or strongest person in my circle to come to terms with the fact that I was addicted to alcohol. It was easier for me to be at ease, perhaps, than someone who walks into an AA meeting alone and facing a wave of people they've never seen.

But I will tell you this. If you're afraid to go to AA, if you believe you don't need it, if you think you're better than all of that—get over it and go. I fought it for a long time. I fought and fought until my therapist told me that she would no longer work with me unless I attended a meeting to see what it was all about.

On my first visit I did the requisite "My name is Meredith and I'm an Alcoholic," and I listened to the stories… And I left feeling much better and more in control of my life than I had in years.

I continued to attend AA meetings. I read the *Big Book* in addition to all of the other alcohol- and addiction-related books I could find. I found great comfort in the structure the meetings provided. I liked the 12 Steps, and the directness with which they addressed alcohol addiction—I didn't feel like I had to hide anything. I dove into the "moral inventory" and the "amends." I liked hearing other people's stories. I stopped short of giving my own testimonial and getting a sponsor, though. I had my therapist and felt that was sufficient.

AA worked wonders for me. The continual repetition of the same principles helped rewire my brain's synapses and altered my thinking about my drinking. The fellowship with other alcoholics made me feel less alone. And sometimes I needed somewhere to go where everyone wasn't drinking.

Alcoholics Anonymous Helped Me:

Find others with whom I could identify so that I didn't feel so alone.

Give structure to my days when I wasn't drinking. I always had somewhere to go if I needed it.

Take a real inventory of the things in my life that made me abuse alcohol.

Admit out loud that I had a problem.

Gain the motivation to take the necessary steps to improve my life.

Get FREE help and assistance at a time when I was feeling really low. The folks in AA practically throw their phone numbers at you. They want you to be connected, get the help you need and to help you stop struggling.

There are 1.2 million AA members in the United States. Going to these meetings immediately connects you to a support group that not only cares about your specific condition but also offers a program with a proven track record of success. Best of all, it's free.

But I eventually stopped going, and here's why.

Even though I recommend that everyone who is reconsidering the role drinking plays in their life should check out AA, I don't continue with meetings myself. After a while, I stopped identifying as an alcoholic. I got fatigued with going in once or twice a week and having to announce to a room full of people that, "I am an alcoholic." At that point, other things in my life had started to become forefront in my mind, like the fact that I was a writer, or a hiker or a good friend. I never got to walk into a room and announce "Hi, I'm Meredith, and I feel really good that I was able to help my friend drive her sick dog to the vet today." Or "Hi, I'm Meredith. I finished my fourth chapter this afternoon." I wanted to shift my thinking to be able to embrace the positive things that were helping me move forward, not continually snap myself back to my alcohol abuse. Because at that point, the only time I was even thinking about alcohol was when I was at those meetings.*

I also started to chafe at the idea that we are powerless over alcohol. I was surrounded by people who were proving, one day at a time, that there was *nothing* over which they were powerless. These were some very powerful, motivated, energetic people. Alcohol is created and marketed to be *extremely powerful*—but no one ever talked about that. We just talked about what we perceived to be our own weaknesses. Were the Native Americans weak because they didn't overcome the attacks on them by the Europeans? Absolutely not. They were just outgunned. And that's how I feel about alcohol. We're not weak. The alcohol companies have much stronger weapons.

I'm not at all opposed to AA, and I keep the idea that there are meetings one block away from my house in my back pocket in case I need it. If my drinking ever escalates to the point where I can't distinguish my bed from my dog's, you better believe I'll go back to those meetings. AA is a remarkable organization that helps people like you and me get back on their feet—and I recommend you go to as many meetings as you can while you decide the role drinking will play in your life.

I have received some feedback since the publishing of this book that not all AA meetings disallow this kind of discussion. This is true. AA meetings are all slightly different depending on where you attend. I strongly encourage you to find meetings that share your values, allow you to feel supported, and help you achieve your goals.

Rehab

Back when I was boozing it up, I used to imagine someone whisking me off to rehab, preferably one of those fancy places in Malibu where I could sleep in, walk on the beach and spend all day talking about my problems. Unfortunately, this didn't happen, so I don't have any first-hand knowledge of what rehab might be like. Plus, I work, and there's no way I could have taken that much time off to focus solely on my sobriety.

But if you want to quit drinking permanently and need this kind of help, I strongly urge you to do it. Rehab is an absolute gift—a luxury that you should allow yourself if you truly want to take on your drinking full steam ahead. Check yourself in, deal with the craziness and see it as the gift that it is. I wish I had been that lucky—lucky enough to step completely out of my life for 30, 60 or 90 days to get my head on straight. As it worked for me, I started with seven days sober here and there, and my journey to sobriety took a lot longer than it probably needed to.

If you're unable to go full time, there are also outpatient options that offer the help you need while you continue to work and live at home. Every city in the country offers something. This should be a relief to you because finding the right program is easy, and it shows that you are clearly not alone. Millions of people struggle with alcohol abuse.

Finding the right rehabilitation center for you should be a simple process of asking around.

Start with your insurance company. If you're fortunate enough to have an insurance plan, check with them first to see what they cover and if they have a facility they work with. My insurance refuses to cover addiction treatments, so I was on my own.

If you're uninsured, check with your local social services programs. They can help you identify the right treatment for you.

Search the Internet. Google rehabs in your area, then call a few to find out what methods they use and talk to staff to see if they are in alignment with your goals.

If you're not covered by insurance, try to negotiate your rate. Work with the treatment center to come up with a lowered rate or payment plan. They are actually in the business of helping people, and many will help you find a way to finance your treatment so that it works for you.

Private Therapy

My therapist saved my life. She was the one who told me that she refused to work with me unless I quit drinking. She took me to my first AA meeting. She helped me clear my body and mind of alcohol so that we could start getting to the roots of why I ended up in therapy with a drinking problem to begin with.

I know a few other people who have tackled their drinking with the work of a private therapist. Some of them didn't last because the fact is that therapy hurts a lot—a LOT—before you start feeling better. I went a couple times a week for over a year before I could walk out of that room feeling anything but miserable. Most people who have a drinking problem aren't willing to go through that, which is probably why they drink in the first place.

But if you can stick it out, private therapy is an invaluable resource to not only understand your drinking, but to understand everything about why you make the choices you make.

Hypnotherapy

I can't say enough good things about hypnotherapy. Finding a qualified hypnotherapist helped me to take the final plunge into my true recovery.

For those of you who may be weirded out by the voodoo aspect of this kind of treatment, I can tell you that all hypnotherapy does is guide you into a state of total relaxation and receptivity to the ideas you yourself develop. I worked with my hypnotherapist to create the suggestions that would work best for my own sobriety. She also explained to me that I could use hypnotherapy to curb bad drinking habits rather than eliminate drinking entirely, but I chose to go the full Monty because it's what I thought would work best for me.

We had a thorough interview where we discussed my problems and my goals and she crafted a hypnotherapy program that used my own words and my own thoughts.

The result was that I was able to step into sobriety in a relaxed, anxiety-free state. That's all. Hypnotherapy shifted my mindset from one of anxiety and feeling overwhelmed to a very calm, focused perspective on my problems and the solutions. Even though I have CD of the sessions I can listen to at any time, I still go back for checkups. Hypnotherapy provides an effortless way to relax, get centered and face your fears about your sobriety with little or no stress.

Online Communities

Connecting with people who have embraced sobriety is easier than ever online. There are hundreds of sites, chat rooms, support groups and blogs online that you can access. I love going online and reading other people's stories and offering them support, especially when they're starting out.

Moderation Management

There are many people who believe that problem drinkers can learn to be moderate drinkers. They refute the idea that the 12-Step, total abstinence method found in AA is the only way to control drinking, and they offer solutions to help curb drinking without eliminating it entirely. I have not personally tried these methods. For me quitting was the best option, but that may not be the case for you. If you've found during your seven days sober that you may be more of a problem drinker than an alcoholic drinker and you'd like to be able to enjoy an occasional adult beverage, this may be the program for you. Like AA, Moderation Management meetings are free of charge and accept anyone who wants to control their drinking. Although I've never attended one of their meetings, I like the idea that they accept that one method doesn't necessarily work for every single person, and they offer an alternative to those who want to avoid AA for whatever reason. You can find information about Moderation Management at moderation.org.

Final Word About Quitting

If you want to quit drinking and you need help, ask for it. There is no reason in the world why you need to tackle this problem on your own.

Deciding Not to Quit

If you decide to keep drinking, I hope you found the clarity you need throughout this process, and have learned some things you may not have known before. I also hope that you can continue to enjoy alcohol responsibly and with pleasure, and that your future experiences with alcohol are healthy, moderate and enjoyable.

No matter how you decide to proceed from this point forward, these seven days were a small beginning. I hope it was useful to you, and I wish you the best of luck on your continued journey.

What My Life Looks Like Now

There was no fanfare for me. There was no dramatic intervention or huge gathering of family or friends celebrating my sobriety. There wasn't even a TV movie-worthy rock bottom, reckoning and recovery. My journey to sobriety was—and still is—a quiet one, one that consists of no big dramas, just small decisions made each hour of each day.

My problems did not go away when I quit drinking. I still get annoyed easily when things don't go my way. I still have a narcissistic mother, an emotionally absent father and a brother who died from addiction. I still suffer from anxieties about work, money and my future. I am still a perfectionist who would sometimes rather quit than look foolish, lie than be wrong or try too hard than have people think I'm lazy. I still try to control everything so that nothing goes awry.

But I am finally aware that none of these things are better served when I am drinking. Drinking until I can't remember, stumbling off to bed and waking up feeling drained and depleted does not make my anxiety go away, my control issues any easier or my mother love me any more. All of the problems in my life that made me drink in the first place are still here, only now I am able to face them clearly, with energy and with greater insight.

If you choose to quit drinking, no matter what your situation is, I promise you that your life will change in ways that you cannot have predicted. You will feel better, look better and have a better frame of mind—all that's a given. But you will also find your world opening up to accommodate dreams that you didn't even know you had. And you'll finally be able to get out of bed early enough to achieve them.

Questions to Consider:

What words would you use to describe your seven days of sobriety?

What was the hardest part? What was the easiest part?

In what ways are you clearer about your drinking? In what ways are you more confused about your drinking?

What was the most important thing you learned about yourself this week?

What was the most surprising discovery while you were sober?

Do you think you'll keep drinking, or explore ways to eliminate alcohol from your life?

What's next for you?

Special Section, Updated for 2020:

Sixty Things to Do While You're Not Drinking

If you're anything like me, all activity comes to a screeching halt once your glass is filled. I can still whip up a snack or maybe fold some laundry, but the truth is that, once I start drinking, that's pretty much what I'm going to be doing until I go to sleep.

Admitting that this is true makes it impossible not to recognize that I have wasted a lot of valuable time in my life passively drinking when I could have been actively pursuing things that interest me. And even though I have realized that my time is better spent doing anything other than slogging down a bottle of wine, I still sometimes have difficulty not getting fidgety when I have a day of unplanned nothing stretching out in front of me.

To make it easier for you, I've come up with a handful of activities that will not only help you keep your mind off drinking, but that may also contribute to your overall sense of accomplishment, your health and your well-being. Try any or all of these in any order you wish.

Take a walk
For my money, taking a walk of any length, in any direction, and in any location, is the very best thing you can do to relieve stress, clear your head and relieve your troubles. If you're not much of a walker, start easy—maybe a stroll around the block or a leisurely saunter in the park. If you can make it brisk, then even better. But I promise you, if you add walking into your daily routine, you'll have more energy, feel less anxious and you'll sleep better. Plus, I love the added bonus of seeing the town where I live up-close. In my daily walks I've discovered wildflower-strewn country lanes, neighbors who keep chickens in their backyards,

hidden gardens and little-used scenic paths. My city walks have led me to indescribably cool boutiques, art-covered alleys and quirky neighborhood watering holes. Walking is the great joy of my life.

Visit some drinking-related websites

There is a wealth of information online about drinking, not drinking, moderate drinking… If you're looking to build a community of support for your decision about drinking, do some Googling to find people who are dealing with the same issues you may be dealing with. I love how online communities can instantly connect me to someone who may be struggling with my exact problem. I also love websites that have informative articles that provide insight into my own drinking issues.

Resources:

Soberistas.com: A great online resource for those who have chosen a life of sobriety, with well-written articles and a feeling of community support.

Learn your local birds

Birds are the only wildlife most of us come into contact with on a daily basis, so it's fitting that we should be able to recognize and identify at least a few of our feathered friends. Plus, birding is not only a fascinating subject to research—you're always learning something new—but it's also a brilliant way to stop and take a moment out of your day to witness nature. Get a book that has information on your local birds, and you can birdwatch (or "bird" as the experts call it) in any setting. I find myself stopping everywhere to see what kinds of birds are around me, and I am instantly brought into the present moment.

Resources:

The Sibley Guide to Birds by David Allen Sibley. Simply the definitive guide for beginning or expert birders.

iBird Explorer App. This incredible tool features photographs, sounds and characteristics of hundreds of birds for easy identification. Sometimes if you play the bird songs in the field, birds will come in close out of curiosity. ibird.com.

Prepare a meal from scratch

With all your free time away from drinking, there's no reason in the world you can't figure out how to make a meal. So many of us rely on takeout or pre-packaged foods to sustain ourselves because cooking either doesn't interest us or we think we can't do it. Or, there are those of us who love to cook, but get stuck making the same things over and over again. If you're the take-out type, I urge you to take back control of your meals. Cooking a simple dish for yourself is easy, fun and more nutritious. If you're a seasoned home cook, why not try something new like creating an entirely vegetarian menu or cuisine from a faraway land?

Clean a drawer, closet or shelf

All journeys worth taking, in my opinion, start with de-cluttering. Piles of junk that accumulate in drawers, closets and shelves not only make things unorganized and unsightly, but I believe the clutter in one's home or office is a reflection of their inner chaos. Clutter is the snake that eats its own tail—clutter is your inner-self acting out its lack of control while in turn making you feel even more out of control of your space. Clear out the things you no longer use that are weighing you down, get those corners cleared and you'll see a difference in how energy flows through your space. Plus, tackling a small, disorganized spot is fast way to feel a huge sense of accomplishment.

Resources:

Unclutterer.com. I love this site for inspiration, tips and great de-cluttering tales.

konmari.com. At the risk of sounding like a band-wagoner, I love, love, love Marie Kondo and I don't care who knows it. Her book, *The Life-Changing Magic of Tidying Up* delivers exactly what is promised. The trick? You have to do the steps exactly like she says. Just because you've tidied a drawer does not mean you have "Marie Kondo'd" your house. It's a prescriptive process, and I cannot recommend her methods highly enough. **PRO TIP:** Remember that her system is about deciding what you *keep* not what to discard. Go spark some joy!

Read

Everyone I know says they wish they had more time for reading, myself included. It doesn't matter whether it's a self-help book, a classic tale or your favorite magazine, use your extra time to curl up with the printed word.

Read books about drinking

In my recovery I've found that reading other people's drinking dramas is one of the most calming, reassuring things I can do. Like the sharing of our stories in AA, reading about the trials and tribulations of drinkers from all walks of life can instantly reaffirm your decision while making you realize that you aren't alone. You're brave for being honest about your drinking, and reading what others have gone through can help bolster you when things look tough.

Resources:

How I Quit Smoking and Drinking and Everything Else I Loved Except Sex, by Susan Shapiro

Recovery by Russell Brand

Drinking: A Love Story, by Caroline Knapp

The Easy Way to Quit Drinking, by Allen Carr

Unwasted: My Lush Sobriety, by Sacha Scobolic

Blackout: Remembering the Things I Drank to Forget, by Sarah Hepola

Parched, by Heather King

Read books about recovery or self-help
The more help you can get, the better. If one area of your life feels out of control, it's likely that several aspects of your life need to be addressed. Don't let that intimidate you. Remember, we're looking for progress, not perfection! Plus, one of the things I've discovered is that if I'm feeling a certain way or have a certain experience, the odds of me being the only person in the world who has ever dealt with it are pretty slim. I always seek books by people who have met life's struggles and found ways to effectively deal with them. Not only do I discover tips and tools, but I also feel a little less alone. I encourage you to find your tribe. Browse the self-help section at your local bookstore and prepare to feel better.

Resources:

The "Big Book," published by Alcoholics Anonymous. The definitive guide to the Twelve Steps.

The Subtle Art of Not Giving a Fuck by Mark Manson. I read this from cover to cover on a train through Colorado, and when I disembarked, I felt better than I had in years.

How to Be an Adult by David Richo. Just what the title says, this book is my go-to when I have some growing up to do.

Your Money or Your Life by Vicki Robin, Joe Dominguez and Monique Tilford. This book has changed many lives, and it has personally helped me focus on what really matters.

The Places that Scare You by Pema Chödron. Learn to face your fears and realities head on in order to move through and eventually past them into a life of greater serenity.

Visit your local library

I discovered my local library on one of my first sobriety walks. Sounds crazy, but I had always ordered books from Amazon or streamed movies on Netflix until I came out from under my rock and learned what everyone else in my town seemed to know—libraries are the best places on the planet. There are books in there! And magazines! And movies! I could spend hours walking through the shelves to see what catches my eye. Head to the library, get a card if you don't have one, and stock up on books and movies to keep yourself entertained. **PRO TIP FOR 2020**: When you bring something home, give it a good wipe down with a disinfectant spray or rubbing alcohol. Not only will the book feel cleaner in your hands, but you're helping the library keep its stock clean and well-maintained.

Discover a new hiking trail

Most towns in America have access to some sort of park or hiking trail. I may be a bit biased on this one since I live in Northern California and you can't swing a dead fish without hitting an amazing regional or state park. If you can find a trail either online or by checking a local trail book out from the library, you're sure to enjoy the journey of discovery into the woods, by the beach, along the stream… Spending time in nature is a smart and affordable way to de-stress during your seven days sober.

Resources:

Trails.com. Simply type in your zip code and you'll be directed to all the trails in your area. Features great information on difficulty level, what to bring and other details that make your trip that much better.

Ride a bike

Rent it, borrow it, buy it used or new—get yourself a bike and remember what it was like to feel the wind in your hair. (Or under your helmet, depending on local laws and your preference.)

Donate

Is there anything more instantly satisfying than cleaning out your closet, cleansing your junk drawer or dumping the detritus in your garage? I say no! I love this plan during the seven days sober program because it provides several things you need to help you re-affix your focus from drinking to reward-based activities: 1) The physical movement required to clear out your clutter can be pretty taxing. Moving those boxes, taking out that trash and loading up the car offers terrific exercise. 2) It's a mental rush to exert control over your space and things. So often our stuff starts to own us, rather than the other way around. Doing a deep clean and de-clutter helps you begin managing your space. 3) And finally, I believe there's a metaphysical payoff to dumping the junk. When your space is cleared, you can be released from any blocked energy that's keeping you stuck.

Resources:

Goodwill.org. To locate a drop-off location or to arrange a pickup, contact the good folks at Goodwill. Make sure your stuff is in good enough condition for them to actually resell. Broken, stained, dirty or ruined items should go in the trash.

Meditate

Everywhere I turn people are encouraging meditation. There's a good reason for that. Meditation is the single best way to reduce anxiety, increase awareness and feel more connected to your own thoughts and emotions. I'm by no means an expert in meditation, but I am usually able to schedule time to meditate every day for a few minutes. Sit still. Breathe. Focus on your breathing. Clear your mind. It's simple, but not necessarily easy. Do it anyway. Just sit there for a few minutes and see what happens. You should be able to find the same amount of time you usually devote to drinking to doing a little meditation here and there.

Resources:
Headspace.com. This site and its smartphone app are all the rage among the pillow-sitters. It's meditation made easy.

Learn a yoga pose or two
Aside from all the hokum-pokum that seems to come along with yoga, there are real physical benefits to a yoga practice. There's a reason it's been popular for thousands of years. Pick up a book of yoga poses or check out a DVD from the library to see how some daily stretching and focused breathing can help structure your day. I've found having a favorite pose or two in my back pocket makes relieving stress instant and easy—and drink free.

Resources:
Rodney Yee's Yoga for Beginners. Rodney makes it easy to love yoga! With training to help you get your form perfect and two full-length yoga workouts, this DVD will inspire you.

YOGA: The Path to Holistic Health by BKS Iyengar. This is a great book to start with. It doesn't have a full practice per se, but there's a detailed index where you can find your specific trouble, be it physical or mental, and the corresponding pose to help alleviate your symptoms.

Youtube.com. Search for yoga videos of any length and difficulty and you will have hundreds of 100% free options to choose from, led by skilled teachers.

Make a smoothie

Delicious, nutritious and fun to make, especially if you fancy yourself a mix-master, smoothies are a great way to get a little energy boost while still feeling like you're drinking something special.

Resources:

Allrecipes.com and Smoothierecipes.com. Smoothies galore! There are hundreds here to choose from. Find your favorite flavorful choices and get blending.

Volunteer

Most of us, at one point or another, have claimed that we would like more time to volunteer, and nearly everyone has a cause that interests them. I'm not saying you have to go work at a soup kitchen every night, but you could offer to help the organization of your choice send emails, make fundraising calls, stuff envelopes, clean out cages… There are limitless ways for you to get involved if you take the time to do a little research.

Manage your finances

While you're getting real about your drinking, I highly recommend you get real about your finances. Take some time to set up your bills for automatic bill pay through your bank's website. Create an action plan to tackle your debt. Or, if you're debt free, set up an interest-bearing savings account online, and have the money automatically withdrawn from your checking account each month. Find and consolidate 401(k) plans or IRAs that you may have from previous employment. Create a budget and stick to it. Spending a few evenings getting on top of your financial situation will not only bring you into a sense of control, but it will also help you prepare for your future in a mature and realistic way.

Resources:

> **mrmoneymustache.com.** This blog is a revelation. Mr. Money Mustache has hacked the system to create a debt-free life of profound self-reliance, freedom and joy. It's not a financial management blog as much as it is an excellent example of an aspirational lifestyle— one that anyone can achieve.

Write a letter

Is there anything more fun than getting an actual letter in the mail? Surprise someone you love with a correspondence other than email. Pick out the paper, write your thoughts with a pen, fold it carefully and place it in a stamped envelope. Walk to your nearest letterbox and drop it in. It's a lovely way to spend a few hours and to make the recipient feel incredibly special.

Plan a trip

In his book published in 1896, *Smoking and Drinking* author James Parton writes "The French have a verb—*se dépayser*—to uncountry oneself, to get out of the groove, to drop undesirable companions and forsake haunts that are too alluring by going away for awhile, and, in returning, the old friends and habits." He recommends that people struggling with alcohol abuse get out of the rut. Take a road trip, bus tour or a plane ride to somewhere you've never been. Surround yourself with new people, new foods and new experiences. If you've got the means, make this trip your reward for completing your seven days. Whether it's a weekend away or a month-long holiday, going somewhere new always helps to shift perspective, especially if you're re-evaluating how—and with whom—you spend your time. **PRO TIP FOR 2020:** Create a staycation around your home territory. Watch a video about National Parks online. Read about someone's harrowing journey into nature.

Resources:

A Walk in the Woods by Bill Bryson. Follow one of our most beloved writers on a journey through the Appalachian Trail.

Wild by Cheryl Strayed. Here's a gal who has struggled with some capital-S "Stuff." She gets her shit together, puts it in a backpack and heads out, alone, on a life-changing trek up the Pacific Crest Trail.

Take a tour

I fell in love with the free, docent-led walking tours in San Francisco when I was first attempting sobriety. Spending an afternoon walking through a beautiful city learning fascinating historical facts, discovering hidden corners and meeting new people was a really fun and easy way for me to get out of my own head. I've also participated in tours at local regional parks, farms, museums and more. See if there are any tours you can join in your area—so many great tours are free or very inexpensive. Plus, there are several companies right now that offer downloadable audio tours that you can do at your own leisure. I found these to be particularly helpful when I traveled to cities for business and didn't want to end up in the hotel bar. Step out on a tour rather than stepping up to the bottle!

Resources:

Detour.com. Amazing, fascinating, wonderful downloadable tours of all your favorite cities. Put them in your smartphone and hit the road. You'll love all of the interesting background information, hidden gems and off-the-beaten track joys you'll discover with these clever tours.

Go to dinner alone

Treat yourself to fancy meal at a place you've always wanted to try, or head down to your favorite neighborhood hangout for a quick bite. The point is to enjoy a meal in public by yourself. Take a book or take time out to spy on the diners around you. I've always found that dining by myself doesn't make me feel like a need a drink with dinner. I also like the way going solo to a restaurant gets me out of my routine and allows me to think quietly about the recent events in my life. It doesn't hurt that there's a nice server bringing me stuff, and that I don't have to do dishes.

Binge an entire season of your favorite TV show

If you're doing your seven days sober during the rainy/wintry/crappy weather season, there's no better way to pass a dreary day than plopped in front of the tube. I'm usually not a huge advocate for TV-watching, but in this case, I recommend it. I have discovered that rainy Saturdays are a real temptation for uncorking several bottles of my favorite wine, but if I can get absorbed in what my favorite characters are up to I can stave off the cravings.

Plant a garden (or a pot)

Get your hands dirty! Putting some plants in the ground and then dedicating yourself to making them grow is a wonderful, nurturing activity. If you don't have a yard, it's still easy to get your garden on with a container garden. Grow plants you eat or plants you love to look at. Either way you're beautifying your backyard, perking up your patio or decking out your deck with an eye-catching addition that's actually alive.

Resources:
> **Sunset National Garden Book,** by Sunset Publishing. Every gardener I know swears by Sunset. It's the most complete resource you'll find for planting successfully in your "zone."

Exercise

I highly recommend you get some form of exercise anytime you take a break from drinking, and even when you don't.

Getting a good workout is the single best thing you can do to alleviate stress, make your heart healthy and to feel like you've accomplished something worthwhile. And you don't need to join a gym to get a great workout. Check out some workout DVDs, find some faves on YouTube or commit to doing 20 minutes of jumping jacks every day. Get your booty moving. You might even lose a few pounds!

Start a blog

Blogging is an easy and affordable way to share your experiences, and to discover a community of people who share your interests. One possible topic, of course, is your experience choosing sobriety over sloppiness. But you could blog about married life, single life, simplifying your life, cooking, shopping, entertainment, eating—anything that interests you or any topic in which you have some expertise.

Resources:

> **Wordpress.com.** Set up a free account with this service and you'll be blogging before you know it. Great-looking templates, easy-to-understand tutorials and simple guides bring blogging within reach of even the least techno-savvy among us.

Learn a craft

I'll have to admit that I personally don't have any experience with this because I hate crafting. But… So many people I know love to knit, sew, alter books, paint and so many other things that crafting seems like a very positive way to spend your time. Do you want to get hooked on crochet? Do it! Take a stab at knitting? What's stopping you? And remember—you probably won't be good at it right away, but stick to it anyway. Anything worth doing is worth doing well, and doing anything well takes a whole lot of practice.

Don't get a pet

You're feeling good, you're in control, you've cleaned out your garage, managed your finances and gotten clear about your drinking. You need a pet! No. You don't. If you have picked up this book it's because you are questioning something in your life in regards to your own choices, attitudes, perceptions and experiences. Do not quit drinking and then avoid all of the self-care you require by bringing home another creature whose needs will overshadow your own. If you want something to cuddle, cuddle yourself. If you need something to walk, be my guest and walk yourself. An animal is a living being that requires enormous attention, care and stability. You need to focus on yourself. It's not fair to the dog, cat, hedgehog or ferret to bring them into a situation where they may get lots of love, but maybe not the focused routine they deserve. Don't get a pet.

Call a long-lost friend

I love Facebook for effortlessly connecting me with all of my buddies from past years. But it's also important to connect with people in a less digital way. Maybe it's time to call someone you knew before you started drinking. Perhaps you can relive all those silly moments you shared before alcohol became the driver. Maybe you know someone who remembers the young, hopeful, little-kid you and they can help you get in touch with that child who loved baseball or singing in the choir. Set an appointment if you have to, but call an old friend and try to remember yourself in a different way.

Call your mother

This can be kind of a minefield, I know. But sometimes when we get distracted with our lives we forget to stay in touch with the people who raised us. Call your mom while you're sober to see how she's doing. You don't have to tell her about your drinking or your sobriety. Have a chat. It will mean a lot to her.

Play a non-video game
Scrabble, Trivial Pursuit, cards, horseshoes, croquet, flag football, bocce ball… There are infinite choices as far as games are concerned. I've even seen some enterprising young people creating their own Quidditch tournaments. Have some fun!

Resources:
Wingspan. Admittedly, I love this one because I am a birder, but you don't have to know about or even like birds to find this strategy game compelling and thought-provoking. The added bonus is that it's beautiful to look at.

Scopa. This ancient Italian card game is so weird and fun that it's impossible to not enjoy yourself. Good for all ages.

Play with your kids
When we're busy parenting (read: making sure the homework's done, shuttling them back and forth between practices, getting those teeth brushed and the laundry put away) it's so easy to forget that having a family is supposed to be fun. In my heavy drinking days I couldn't wait for the kids to get into bed so I could play with my best friend chardonnay. Take some time to play with your kids. If Barbie or Legos aren't your thing, that's ok. Teach your kids to cook something. Wrestle. Play a game. Draw some pictures. Your kids will love you for it.

Attend a friend's sporting event
You've probably got buddies who are in some sort of sports league or on a team. Go to one of their games. Cheer them on. Make them feel special and appreciated. You might also find that you get into the competitive spirit yourself. I've attended a few adult sporting events and they always inspire me to be more active, and to continue to pursue the things I loved doing as a kid.

Try something new

There's something out there that you've always wanted to try. Try it now! I took up figure skating at age 36. I went surfing for the first time at age 32. I learned to play a couple of tunes on the ukulele. All of these things require complete sobriety, believe me. Maybe you'd like to go play paintball, learn to build websites or audition for a play. It's all out there waiting for you. You just have to put the bottle back on the shelf and do something else instead.

Make a movie

It's so easy to make your own films now! Spend the next seven days writing a script, filming it and posting it online! Make it a comedy or a tragedy. Make it a music video. Make it a TikTok. Whatever you decide, get started on day one and keep going until you finish editing on day seven. Use it for your holiday greeting.

Compose a song

If you're musical, spend your week writing a little ditty or two. Often when we drink, not only does the alcohol blot out our artistic natures, but we don't have the energy to devote to the types of activities that help us express our feelings. Write a song that delivers an emotional punch, makes you laugh or relaxes you.

Go to a poetry or literature reading

For amateur writers, local readings are the only chance they have to share their work. Going to a local reading is usually free, usually in a bookstore (no temptation there) and offer a great way to inspire yourself to put pen to paper to tell your own story.

DON'T spend a lot of money on hobby-related equipment

Now is not the time to throw yourself headlong into an expensive hobby. Do not, in your first fervor of sobriety, drop a lot of cash on that waterski boat, the complete home recording studio or top-of-the-line golf equipment you've always wanted. Take it slow. Try a few simple things to recharge your batteries. Take some time out for simple pleasures. It's your chance to reflect and make some changes, not go balls-to-the-wall on the latest extreme sport, moneymaking hobby or trendy pastime.

Visit a relative
Make some plans to spend the afternoon with an aunt or uncle you haven't seen in a while. Call up your cousin. Spend some time together walking through a park, having lunch or chatting on the phone. Sometimes reconnecting with people who have known us our entire lives helps us reconnect with our spirit—the true spirit inside of us that has been hidden by our drinking. Find a family member to help you find that connection again. **PRO TIP FOR 2020**: Use Facetime or Zoom to stay in touch.

Work late
If you like to get your drink on during the week, chances are you've shown up to work tired, drained and ready to get the heck out of there. The University at Buffalo's Research Institute on Addiction recently released a study that shows that nine percent of American workers are nursing hangovers on the job. In my drinking days, I could easily say that I spent only about nine percent of workdays NOT nursing a hangover. Those non-hangover days were incredibly productive. Use your sober time to stay late and catch up on correspondence, clean out your desk or dump old emails. File the expense reports that were piling up, or sketch out some ideas for saving your department money. If you're working from home, stay connected a little later, take on a project for a colleague or be the cheerleader to keep the team engaged. It's important to spend your sober week accomplishing things of value.

Clean up your computer

Digital detritus clogs our computers, slows them down and makes it more difficult to retrieve things you need. Take control of your computing by spending a couple of hours making new files, dumping old ones and clearing out your inbox. Update your bookmarks so your favorite sites are easier to find. Sign up for RSS feeds for the blogs you read on a regular basis. Clear out the ones you no longer follow. Create folders in your email program to store information that needs to be saved to keep your inbox clear. Then, swab your disgusting keyboard with rubbing alcohol.

Get a checkup

Neglecting your health goes with the territory when you're drinking too much. Schedule a visit with your doctor over the next seven days. Get a checkup and some blood work. You can explain that you're interested in curbing your drinking, and see what resources are available through the medical community. It's your decision. But it's a good idea to actually know what's going on with your body before you make any sort of lasting call about whether or not you want to continue drinking. **PRO TIP FOR 2020:** So many doctors will respond to emails or do online video conferencing to discuss minor issues. Even though the wait times might be a bit long, don't hesitate to contact your doctor for anything that concerns you.

Get a makeover

Head to your nearest department store, sit yourself down at the makeup counter and let the professionals have at it. You can usually get a free makeover with no obligation to buy. It's fun to have someone fawn over you for a half hour, and then to see how pretty you look! You might catch a glimpse of what the sober you would look like if you were to get dolled up for a night of healthy fun. Or, you could discover a whole new way to enhance your best features for your workday. **PRO TIP FOR 2020**: Choose from one of thousands of makeover videos online and practice on yourself.

Have a massage
Book it! With the money you're saving on booze this week, you should treat yourself to a therapeutic massage. Kneading your tired, stressed out muscles releases the toxins that have built up in your system, realigns joints that may be out of whack and eliminates stress in a way that requires nothing from you but lying there. Totally relaxing and utterly healthy, a good massage should be at the top of your list of activities this week.

Clean out the fridge/pantry/laundry room
There are a lot of de-cluttering suggestions on this list. That's because I believe wholeheartedly that our external spaces often reflect our internal makeup. And I also believe that organized, clutter-free spaces leave us less stressed, more able to think and process and keep the energy flowing freely. So get in there and clean out the old, rotten food, wipe down the counters and freshen up your space. Not only will you feel energized, but your home will begin to feel like a calming retreat as opposed to a war zone.

Fly a kite
Simple, elegant, timeless. I bought a mini butterfly kite for under $5. It's about five inches long and it fits in my car's glove box. On a breezy day, I can stop at a park and spend a half hour flying my silly little kite. It's so engrossing that the stress of the day melts away. Plus, it's such a tiny kite that I inevitably get people asking me about it. Flying a kite is a joyous way to disconnect from stress and reconnect with your inner child all at once.

Support local theater
There's something very communal and wholesome about going to a local theater event. Oftentimes the players are people you know or know of. I recently watched our local

school superintendent sing and dance, and our police chief crack wise. More often than not, your local actors, singers and dancers are better than you ever imagined. Head out for an evening of entertainment not provided by the black box in your living room. You'll be pleasantly surprised.

Go to the farmer's market

One of the hallmarks of my own drinking past was my unwillingness to connect with others. I hated shopping because I couldn't stand the supermarket—it was full of people, I had to talk to the checkout folks and I was always embarrassed by the amount of booze in my cart. What a nightmare. When I began to eat healthier and drink less, I discovered my local farmer's market. Not only did I learn about vegetables I'd never heard of, I also became aware of the importance of eating certain things when they were in season, and I found a fun way to combine a morning walk with my shopping. Shopping for nourishment became a fun adventure rather than an inconvenient hassle.

Go to church

If you're feeling lost and alone, head to a church service. I recommend this whether you're religious or not. Try a Christian church, a Jewish temple, a Quaker meeting or a Buddhist meditation—it doesn't really matter. Being in a quiet place surrounded by people who have gathered to hear an uplifting message can be enough to get you through a lonely time. You may discover that you enjoy the congregation and come back for more. You may see that this particular church isn't for you, but you're interested in finding something that works—or you may confirm that church isn't your thing. No matter what you decide, you will have filled more than an hour of your non-drinking time with something that's, for the most part, positive. **PRO TIP FOR 2020**: Find a service you can connect to live online.

Groom yourself

Tweeze those brows, paint those toes, wax that area…
Spend a little home time getting yourself feeling good and
in ship shape. Put a conditioning mask on your hair,
exfoliate, use a little self-tanner to bring back your healthy
glow. Treat yourself to all those little details that sometimes
fall through the cracks when we get so busy.

Redecorate your house

And by this I do not mean go out and drop a wad of cash on
reinventing your home. Rearrange your furniture. Buy a
new bedspread. Paint your bedroom that shade of blue
you've always loved. Pull down that ugly wallpaper border
in the bathroom. Change out a light fixture. Hang that
picture you bought two years ago. Arrange some flowers.

Resources:

> **Apartmenttherapy.com**. I love Apartment Therapy for
> clever, affordable inspiration for every room in my
> home.

Have sex

If you've got a willing partner, go for it! Why spend your
newly sober hours fretting about what to do when you can
get busy getting busy? So often our drinking leads to some
frantic, weird sex that we don't remember or appreciate.
Grab your loved one, turn off your phone, dim the lights
and try to remember what it was like to be close to someone
without being buzzed.

Take a nap

All of this personal reflection may be wearing you out.
Years of drinking may have disturbed your sleep patterns.
Or maybe you feel fantastic but want to take a short break
from your day. Close the blinds, tuck yourself in and feel
free to sleep the day away. Napping is a healthful
alternative to an afternoon of drinking and one of the most
decadent things I love to do.

Take a bath
Ahhh, bath time! The best time of the day. Fill your tub
with hot, bubbly water, turn on some soft music, light a few
candles and slip away. One of the easiest and most relaxing
things you can do any time of day to soothe your frazzled
nerves, taking a bath is a reminder to slow down and enjoy
the simple pleasures of life. Tub time is just one of the
many things you should have in your arsenal this week to
help you unwind while you're not drinking.

Feed yourself
Keeping yourself full and healthy while you're not drinking
is one of the most important things you can do. So often
being hungry leads to being angry (or "hangry" as one of
my friends wittily calls it), and being angry leads to a
craving for alcohol. Now this is not to say you should keep
your desk full of donuts. Try to have some healthy snacks
on hand for when your energy dips. Carrot sticks, energy
bars, a hard-boiled egg for protein…

Also make sure you eat full, balanced meals. Enjoy them
slowly—don't wolf down your food. Take some time out to
really experience what you're eating. If you're used to
eating on the fly, try to resist that urge during your seven
days. Slow down to savor your food in a new and deeper
way. It's one of the best ways to stay healthy this week and
always.

Resources:
> **How to Cook Everything, Completely Revised 10th
> Anniversary Edition: 2,000 Simple Recipes for Great
> Food by Mark Bittman.** The bible for cooking!
> There's nothing that's not covered here. You're sure to
> find a few favorites that make it easier than ever to take
> care of your nutritional needs deliciously.

Write a book

Everyone's got a story to tell. And now that you've cleared up your boozy haze, you could take this time to share yours. Whether it's your memoir about growing up the child of circus performers, an account of the time you won the county spelling bee or a darkly comic novel about zombies who take over the airport, now is your chance to do it. Here are a couple of tips to help you:

Write for an hour a day, no matter what. When I first wanted to be a writer I joined a group in San Francisco called the Red Room Writer's Society. The group's philosophy was that talking about writing is not writing, reading about writing is not writing, dreaming about writing is not writing: only writing is writing. So we would get together once a week and write silently for one hour. That's it. No talking. No critiquing. Just writing. And by the end of the year, I had finished my first short novel in 52 hours. The trick is to write whether you're inspired or not. Write for an hour. No big pressure.

Participate in NaNoWriMo. That's short for National Novel Writing Month. It's in November every year and its purpose is to create an online support system for people to finish their own 50,000-word novel in one month. I did it, and it works. Is my novel good? Not remotely. But it's finished! And I was so obsessed with finishing on time that I wasn't tempted to drink.

Resources:
National Novel Writing Month. Nanowrimo.org. Check in at this site to meet other writers who are frantically trying to complete 50,000 words.

Floss

Seems simple enough. During my heavy drinking I'd brush my teeth and wash my face, but I'd forgo the flossing. Now

I use flossing as a bellwether to determine my overall contentment. Don't laugh! If I'm flossing every night before I go to bed this usually means that I'm organized, calm, happy and healthy. Maybe flossing isn't your issue. Perhaps if you shave every day or wash your hair or wipe down the kitchen counter you're doing a-ok. Find your own thing, and pay close attention to the days it happens and the days it doesn't—it could be a great way to touch base with your emotional state.

Create an end of life plan

No one likes to talk about this, but one of the most freeing things I've ever done is create an "In Case of My Death" document. It contains contact information for my parents, my skating coach and my employer, the passwords to my online banking accounts (so that my partner can access the money we share), instructions on where to send the mortgage checks and due dates for recurring bills like my insurance which will still need to be paid after I'm gone, and details on what kinds of payouts I should receive from my health plan and my life insurance. It took me about three hours to compile this information, and it was well worth it. I sleep better knowing that if I pass away unexpectedly my family has all the information they need to keep their lifestyle intact. They'll have enough to worry about without having to dig up all of my Internet passwords.

Go to a movie

When a craving strikes, one of the best ways for me to shift my attention is to take myself to the movies. Watching a film on the big screen is passive, stress-free entertainment. **PRO TIP FOR 2020**: Turn off the lights, close the door and watch a movie you love on your laptop.

Watch movies about addiction

If you think you can get through a movie about alcoholism without craving a drink, watching movies about addiction can really help you feel better about your decision to stop drinking for seven days. Some of my favorites include:

28 Days: A sparkling Sandra Bullock takes a drunken ride on the crazy train and ends up in rehab quite unwillingly. This is kind of a lighthearted take on the severity of drinking, but it has some interesting characters, a happy resolution and Viggo Mortenson.

Clean and Sober: One of the most memorable scenes from this film is when Michael Keaton comes home from rehab, cleans his entire apartment, sits down in his favorite chair and wonders what on earth he's supposed to do now. This is a common feeling for those of us who quit drinking for any period of time. That's why I created this list—to help you have some options to fill that void.

Leaving Las Vegas: A very dark film, based on the author's real experiences as an alcoholic, *Leaving Las Vegas* is the saddest recommendation on this list. Be prepared to be fully exposed to the desperation and desolation that accompanies severe alcoholism.

Julia: If this movie doesn't make you reconsider your "social" drinking, nothing will. I was riveted as I watched the events in Julia's (played by Tilda Swinton) life unfold—all of it directly related to some very bad decisions made as a result of consuming gallons of booze.

Everything Must Go: This one's a slow burn, but it's a good story about a man who faces the consequences for some very bad drinking-related behavior, and gets his life together as a result.

Drink water

Feeling a craving? Getting a little edgy? Snapping at your friends and family? Take a break. Remove yourself from whatever situation is making you feel that way and drink a tall glass of refreshing water. Drink water every morning when you wake up. Drink water with your lunch. Drink water with your mid-afternoon snack. If you have a daily drinking habit, it's highly likely that you have been dehydrating your body for quite a while. Take in as much water as you can during these seven days. Watch your skin regain its glow. Feel the toxins being rinsed from your organs. Give every cell in your body the hydration it needs to function at its fullest. Drink as much water as you can, as often as you can—and take this advice even after you've completed your seven days.

Self-hypnosis

I discovered self-hypnosis when I first decided to quit drinking. Hypnosis audio files usually last about 50 minutes, and they really do impart a sense of relaxation and calm. You can find hypnosis for any topic ranging from cutting down on drinking, quitting smoking, building confidence, losing weight, better sex… Hypnosis is an absolutely simple way to take a moment from your day to reinforce your decision to be healthier in every aspect of your life.

Resources:

> **Hypnosisdownloads.com.** An online treasure trove of well-done, professional hypnosis downloads on an infinite array of topics.

❧

About the Author

Meredith Bell is a writer and a recovering wine industry professional. She is the author of *A Sober Year: Daily Musings on an Alcohol-Free Life, The Sobriety Handbook: What You Need to Know to Get Sober and Stay That Way,* and *Inside the Sober Mind: Mastering the Mindset of Sobriety.* She lives in Sonoma County, California.

Also by Meredith Bell

The Sobriety Handbook: What You Need to Know to Get Sober and Stay That Way

The sober journey can be fraught with emotional upheaval, confusion about program options and fear of the unknown. This easy-to-understand guide takes the mystery out of the work of sobriety, and lets you know exactly what you need to do next.

Inside the Sober Mind: Mastering the Mindset of Sobriety

Some people have been sober their whole lives. Others got sober—and stayed sober—after realizing that alcohol wasn't working for them. They both have one thing in common: They've mastered the sober mindset. By applying the proven principles in this book, you will transform your thought process into a Sober Mind, and kick your habit forever.

A Sober Year: Daily Musings on an Alcohol-Free Life

Designed to provide daily support to those who have embarked on a sober journey, A Sober Year inspires with personal anecdotes, tips, revelations and observations about sobriety.

Printed in Great Britain
by Amazon